SPIRITUAL INTELLIGENCE

How Your Spirit Will Lead You
To Health, Happiness and Success

Barbara Halcrow, MSW

Spiritual Intelligence
How Your Spirit Will Lead You to Health, Happiness and Success

Copyright © 2011 by Barbara Halcrow
All Rights Reserved.
Unauthorized duplication or distribution is strictly prohibited.

ISBN 10: 0-9831698-5-3
ISBN 13: 978-0-9831698-5-7

Published by: Expert Author Publishing
http://expertauthorpublishing.com

Canadian Address
1265 Charter Hill Drive
Coquitlam, BC, V3E 1P1
Phone: (604) 941-3041
Fax: (604) 944-7993

US Address
1300 Boblett Street
Unit A-218
Blaine, WA 98230
Phone: (866) 492-6623
Fax: (250) 493-6603

"Barbara Halcrow has lived fiercely and deeply the truths of her life. With radiant integrity and not a hint of self pity or posturing she offers her painful early history as proof that even the profoundly wounded can heal. With clarity, compassion and joy she teaches how to use traumatic events as a way to awaken and transform oneself. In this path, there are no victims. This book can awaken the heroes in us all."
Leslie Hamson, North Words Consulting Writer, Teacher of Writing Meditations for Healing

"For all those struggling to find wisdom and grace in their life, read this book! Through compelling personal stories and the benefit of years of psychological and emotional learning, Barbara Halcrow gives us the gift of her deep understanding of spirituality and well-being."
Beverly Cramp, Author, Freelance Writer and Memoirist

"The author's experiences as she grew up in an abusive, dysfunctional family, her journey of self discovery and spiritual awakening, are a lesson for all of us. How she learned to cope by finding her inner strength, and finally channelled that strength and spirituality in order to help others, is truly a remarkable and inspiring journey."
W. Ruth Kozak, Life Writing Instructor, Travel Journalist, and Historical Fiction Writer
www.ruthkozak.com

"Spiritual Intelligence" is a personal straight from the heart account of the author's inspiring and courageous journey toward personal empowerment. The author reveals many spiritual insights and personal healing processes she used to show you how she successfully overcame many of life's challenges. This is a thought-provoking book that can benefit us all by showing us how to connect to our own spirituality".

Bob Burnham, Author of the # 1 Amazon Best Seller
101 Reasons Why You Must Write A Book:
How To Make A Six Figure Income By Writing & Publishing Your Own Book
www.ExpertAuthorPublishing.com

"Barbara Halcrow brings you into the most intimate moments of her life and shows you how to transform terror into a moment of awakening; an opportunity for growth. So you can trust that the myriad tools and teachings you will receive in this book have real power, as they've been forged out of the fire of her own inner alchemy."

Dr. Anne McMurtry
Reiki Master, Crystal Healer and Channeller
Vancouver, BC

This writing is dedicated to my mother, Shirlee, and my father, Gordon, both in spirit, who had extraordinary life journeys. They also had their own gifts, strengths and courage and they gave me many of my hardest life lessons in love, compassion and forgiveness.

To my dearest brother Rob, in spirit. I know you know and you continue on. To my Aunt Catherine, in spirit, whose soul's unconditional love and preciousness was always recognized and appreciated.

To my own soul's courage and vitality in my connection to Spirit, the Divine Intelligence that has governed my life with strength, precision, truth and tenderness, and continues to infuse me with everything I need to know to go forward, in eternity.

ACKNOWLEDGEMENTS

I want to thank all those souls, present and in spirit, who have come onto my path, no matter the measure of our time together—whether lovers, partners, family, friends or colleagues. You have all been part of the fabric of my life and of this book. I am grateful for the love, the learning and the lessons.

To my sister, Lindsay Barber, who has been with me since the earliest years in loving support and outrageous hilarity as she carved out her own amazing life.

To my Aunt Jean Halcrow, who took me to Egypt on a journey back to my spiritual roots and who's supported this work with her generous heart.

To Dr. Anne McMurtry, a kindred spirit who has brought much healing into my life.

I also want to thank Bob Burnham for his support and mentorship of this book. It was all meant to be.

TABLE OF CONTENTS

INTRODUCTION   xiii

CHAPTER 1 - THE EARLY YEARS   1

Family Constellation	2
Parents' Challenges	3
My Arrival	4
My Mantra	5
Early Awakenings	5
Staying Alert	6
Creativity	7
Childhood Heroes	8
Sent Out	9
Deciding to Remember	9
The Eldest Daughter	10
The Power of Encouragement	13
The Mask of Denial	14
The Athlete Emerges	15
The Second House	16
The Importance of Allies	17
My Connection with Spirit	19
Fighting Back	22
"Pass the Humour, Please!"	23
Another Decision	24
The Counsellor Appears	25
"This One's for Me!"	28
Black Widow Haunting	30
Facing My Fears	32
Power Animals	33
Sexual Abuse	34
The Nest Empties	36

My Brother's Return to Spirit	37
Career Beginnings	40
My Father Goes to "Jail"	40
Spirituality and Sexual Identity	44
Re-opening the Wounds	47
Owning My Anger	48
Moving On	49
Some Resolution in Death	50
Into the Fire	53
More Transitions	53
CHAPTER 2 - OPENING YOUR HEART	**55**
Deciding to Open	55
Giving is Receiving	56
Gratitude	57
Prayer	58
Sending Prayer to Another	59
Many Expressions of Love and Healing	61
CHAPTER 3 - YOUR HEART'S DESIRES	**65**
Our Beliefs	65
Our Thoughts	67
Power in Words	68
Create a List of What You Want	69
Imagination	70
Affirming Your Desires	71
Letting Go	72
Be Ready to Receive	72
Setting Time Aside	73
Maintaining Silence	73
Dealing with Doubt	75

CHAPTER 4 - ALLOWING AND TRUSTING — 77

Synchronicity — 78
Our Guiding Inner Voice — 80
Meditation — 81
Dreams — 82
Dream Journals — 85
Guiding Entities — 85
What Helped in that Moment? — 87
Inner Guidance and Divine Intervention — 89
Relationship with Animals — 91
Psychics — 92
Astrology — 93

CHAPTER 5 - YOUR CONSCIOUSNESS AS CONDUIT — 95

Attachments — 96
Being Truthful About Feelings — 98
Abandonment — 99
Acceptance and Forgiveness — 100
Being Present — 104
The Mind/Body Connection — 105
Keeping a Positive Attitude — 110

CHAPTER 6 - TRANSFORMING TO WHOLENESS — 113

Accepting Our Shadow Side — 114
Mirrors — 115
Personal Responsibility — 116
Intimate Relationships — 117
A Higher Perspective — 121

EPILOGUE - LOVE IS BEING — 125

BIBLIOGRAPHY — 129

INTRODUCTION

This story is my own.

It is about being spiritually guided since my early childhood, through extraordinary and dangerous times. By using my courage and staying open to Spirit's knowledge and direction, I faced down my fears, and healed and transformed my life to greater peace, success and happiness.

As a healer and Social Worker I have had the privilege of working with clients and colleagues who have also been wonderful teachers. Life is ultimately about relationships. People enter our lives for specific reasons—to teach us what we need to learn, if only for a few moments or perhaps over a lifetime.

My experiences have shown me that potent, loving energies indeed surround us; that divine intervention, synchronicity and the realm of spirit, dreams and the unseen, are very real and meaningful. We can indeed expand our awareness and see beyond our present physical limitations of time and space to the great energetic richness that surrounds us and is a natural part of our selves.

In sharing my life's journey with you, I want you to know that you can transition from fear and confusion by opening to your own spirit's intelligence—your own inner guidance that can lead you to the peace, success and the happiness that you deserve.

And while there are times we may choose to travel our paths in necessary solitude to access deeper truths, we are truly never alone.

CHAPTER 1

THE EARLY YEARS

My soul's calling has always been to help others heal themselves.

We all have invaluable life journeys to speak of and we are all survivors in some way. I am similar to the many who have lived with parents who were violent, had mental health illnesses and were heavily addicted to alcohol. I found my life initially chaotic and terrifying, with many hurdles to overcome; however, my life has also been enriched with the rewards I received from the spiritual depth of my learning and in facing down the things that frightened me.

Love, compassion and acceptance of myself and others in this life's journey have allowed me to go further in greater empathy and attunement to people's feelings and their needs. This kind of clarity and focus becomes invaluable in offering support and healing to others.

Family Constellation

I was born second in a lineup of four children. Next to my brother, Rob, I am the eldest daughter. I have two sisters, Lindsay and Catherine. We were all raised in Penticton, British Columbia.

My father, Gordon, was a handsome lawyer, with wavy reddish hair, a brilliant mind and a terrific sense of humour. He was a strong legal advocate for Aboriginal rights. He understood the First Nations Peoples culturally and spiritually and he spent much time with them throughout his life.

Gordon came from a well-known Scottish/Viking clan of seven boys and five girls who grew up appreciating hardships as well as successes. His parents came from the very North of Scotland and the Shetland Islands. His father was a well-respected Royal Canadian Mounted Police (RCMP) Chief in Penticton for many years. His mother was a kind, soft-spoken woman who had once cooked with the chef who worked for King Edward VI. Her skills were well utilized with that large, active clan. He grew up in Nelson and Penticton, BC. While in Penticton, Gordon became part of the BC Dragoons Pipe Band. He and his brothers were notable pipers.

My mother, Shirlee, was a remarkably beautiful woman, with big blue eyes, auburn hair and a broad smile that could light up a room. She was the eldest daughter of three girls. Shirlee was a sensitive and very intuitive woman who loved animals, people and all plant life. She loved to cook. She had a charismatic, magnetic energy that was easily felt when you met her. Shirlee was stylish, charming and well cultivated in the social graces. Her father was the manager of the Seed Division of Buckerfields in Vancouver at one time, and her mother was a school teacher. She grew up in Kerrisdale, Vancouver.

Parents' Challenges

Both of my parents were severe alcohol abusers. My mother also had a bipolar-schizophrenic mental health issue that was exacerbated by her alcohol abuse. She was tormented by hallucinations (usually religious in nature), paranoia, confusion, severe depression, violent outbursts and sexual inappropriateness. She had periods of wellness, but they seemed to last for only a few weeks at a time.

Gordon drank too much for most of his life and would never completely stop. His World War II years took their toll on him. He never fully recovered from the trauma and the death of his comrades around him. His despair seemed to revolve particularly around his plane crash off the BC coastline, when his men were trying to come into the Abbotsford airfield in BC. A bomb exploded in his plane, killing several men and dumping the rest into the ocean. His men eventually drowned around him, but Gordon was a strong swimmer and was finally able to make it to shore.

As Gordon's alcoholism continued, his public displays of inebriation increased. These and his subsequent abandonment of his responsibility as a husband and father became fodder for the professional circles in town and newspaper articles. One time his van was found "abandoned with man missing," much to our despair and humiliation when we read about it along with everyone else. He was also known to reside with other women and support their children, while his family had to resort to being assisted by Income Assistance or "welfare."

However, Shirlee and Gordon were far greater people than the illnesses they suffered. They had aspirations, dreams, heartaches, losses and longings. They had love they wanted to give. They had strengths, triumphs, successes, wisdom, spirituality and a sense of their own special gifts. They both wanted to be happy and they wanted to be happy with each other. These desires were never realized.

In spite of the hardships and tests that would come to each one of us in this family, my parents, whom I loved, were two of my greatest teachers.

My Arrival

After my brother Rob was born, I came on board 16 months later. I was born premature at three pounds, 11 ounces. So right off the hop, so to speak, things were not going so well. I was put in an incubator for a month. In those days premature babies didn't survive as easily. Of course I made it because I came from hardy, brave Viking stock and nothing stops us except a case of bad brew, and even then, not always.

My father told me I was up and running in just over six months after I got home. It was a good thing I knew how to run as I'd need some good hooves to try and outrun the abuse that was coming my way.

My Mantra

In the first four to six years of my life, and when my mother was giving birth to my siblings, I was placed for a few weeks with several of my father's sisters: Joan, Cae and Marjorie.

I do remember, at about age four, my Aunt Cae attempting to dress me. I loudly insisted, "I can do it! I can do it myself!" They remind me to this day about this stubborn, independent part of my personality that rose up constantly whenever someone tried to assist me with anything. Although I was more like a shy rabbit then, I seemed to be very determined to loudly proclaim my independence and skills.

"I can do it!" became my own personal power mantra for every challenge I faced for the rest of my life. I meant it every time I said it. And I said it a lot.

Early Awakenings

Daily, I can remember the screaming and fighting between my parents. Shirlee had a good right arm with the ongoing tossing of pots and pans, utensils … just anything handy. I recall that often-joked-about and practically revered, dinged-up electric kettle that flew around the room—like it had its own flight path right to Dad's head.

I knew the neighbours could all hear my parents' fights. I would leave the house when it got really violent and stand outside in the driveway. In the summertime everyone was outside and I could see the neighbours looking at me, whispering and nodding to each other, then turning away to continue their conversations. I felt ashamed and humiliated in those moments. I wanted it all to stop. No one came forward to stop it. A part of me did not understand.

Early morning, when I was five years old, I heard Shirlee and Gordon arguing about someone in their bedroom. Dad suddenly went into the bathroom next to my room and I heard him crying. He sounded distraught, talking out loud, asking Shirlee why she had stabbed him with a knife in his leg. I had never heard my father cry like this before.

This would also be the first incident in my memory where I would know that besides utensils, ashtrays, pans and that proverbial kettle, that knives would be added to the repertoire of weapons that Shirlee would use in her violent threats. It was important to stay alert.

Staying Alert

As children, we became very alert while growing up in our parents' war zone. We learned to be adept at scanning our environment to see if it was safe to venture out of our rooms. We became extremely good observers of human behaviour. We got to know the subtle nuances of our parents. We got to know that if mother has two drinks, it's safe to talk to her and ask for simple favours. If it was more than that, then we ran the risk of her turning on us instantly with her "Jekyll/Hyde" personality changes. A difference in mother's tone, a glance, her widening eyes, an eyebrow twitch, a change in breathing or a slight posture shift meant the difference between being assaulted or staying unharmed.

It became a valuable skill in later life, being that tuned in. You can essentially assess anyone at a distance. "Safe or not safe?" However, being so hyper-vigilant or on "Code Orange" for extended periods of time is to remain in high anxiety and it is extremely stressful. It can become part of your general response system and, over time, it can take its toll on anyone's health, as it did on mine. I battled long periods of insomnia and severe eczema for eighteen years until I left home. Then I was left for many years to work through post traumatic stress and a disruptive anxiety disorder.

In my earlier childhood years, I spent a lot of time in my room. Other times I was outside discharging my energy playing Kick the Can or Red Rover with neighbourhood kids on that big oval park on Windsor Avenue. I hung out a fair bit with my brother, Rob, and a few of his friends. They were always doing adventurous, exciting things like building forts and playing with mechanical objects.

Creativity

Children are naturally creative. When I was alone I would make things with scraps of paper, plastic or wood. I was quite artistic and creative. I loved to draw animals and nature. I would build detailed doll houses from boxes, pieces of wood and popsicle sticks and I would make hand-sewn clothes for my dolls. I would use a small saw from my father's tool area in the basement and make toy boats. Whatever looked interesting in back alleys or around the house, I'd pick it up and make something. I liked using my hands and I enjoyed the concentration and the detail in it all. I loved being involved in my own world, not thinking about anything else. It was a good escape, too.

Childhood Heroes

Before we can ever know we are really our own heroes, childhood heroes can be important.

I never had any real-people heroes around me, so I paid attention to the ones on TV. Heroes like Davy Crockett and Daniel Boone had jingles to them that sang of their fearlessness, braveness and boldness. I wanted to be brave and bold too. I would sing those jingles all the time not knowing I was probably helping to affirm the braveness within myself, because courage and braveness were needed.

One day, my hero-worshiping and creativity went a bit sideways.

When my mother was entertaining a few of the lawyers' wives, I went searching for more of anything to create. I found her Kotex menstrual pads in the bathroom beside the usual assortment of empty liquor bottles. With that entire load of cotton batten to work with, I knew I'd hit the jackpot!

I decided to be my hero, Davy Crockett for the day. I taped together a big white Davy Crockett "racoon skin" hat complete with big white tail attached at the back. On my head it went; although rather large, it was a good fit. I was sure my mother would be pleased with my efforts.

I quietly manoeuvred myself out to her group of friends who were sipping whatever they had in their "teacups." The looks of complete shock greeted me, much to my bewilderment.

"My God, look at her head!" one yelled, pointing at me – "What is THAT? Shirlee, is she ALL RIGHT!?"

I suppose I resembled a child with a serious head injury, except for the white tail flouncing around at the back. Much to my disappointment I was promptly escorted back into my bedroom with serious instruction to *never* touch whatever that was I'd gotten into! My hat was taken away, not to be resurrected again.

Sent Out

"Get out of here and don't come back!" Mom said to me. I was six years old. I had no idea what I had done that had made her so angry with me and she seemed angry with me every day. She repeated her words and pointed to the door. "Don't ever come back!" I remember how hurt and scared I felt and I knew I had to go.

I went outside and looked up the street. I knew where the little grocery store was around the corner with the nice Chinese man, but that was about it. I didn't know what to do. Her words were stinging inside me, "don't ever come back."

I began to walk up the sidewalk. I stopped for a few seconds and looked at my checkered shorts, my pink top and my running shoes with tiny strings of colours running through them. I looked down at the sidewalk and noticed the little pieces of grass that were growing out of the cracks in the cement. I noticed the pieces of flattened gum and tar, too. I felt the summer's heat. It was a sunny, blue-sky day with barely a breeze.

Deciding to Remember

Then I made a decision. I told myself I would remember all of this. I would remember everything. I *had* to. I had to memorize everything so I wouldn't get lost. I walked up the street, studying all my footsteps, wondering, "Who is going to look after me?" "Where am I supposed to go?"

My walk seemed to take forever. I got to the top of the street and looked to the right toward the little grocery store. It was too far. I would have to cross the street and I was too afraid. I knew I had to turn back. I had no choice. I wondered, "How do I get back into the house?"

Then it came to me. I would just tell her I was sorry. I didn't know sorry for what but I would have to make myself say that. I finally got to the front door where she was. I opened the screen door carefully and blurted out my sentence, "Mommy, I'm sorry!" Her blue eyes stared straight ahead as she kept chopping something at the counter. It worked. I ran to my room.

With this decision I'd made to visually memorize when I needed to, I would develop my mind over the years quite well to take "snapshots" of people and places, and then later on, pages of information at school. It would be a skill that helped keep me focussed within the chaos, fear and confusion at home.

The Eldest Daughter

"Barbara, you are responsible." It was a clear message from my mother and it was not to be argued with. I was eight years old and I was responsible for my two youngest sisters no matter what they did or where they were. I was responsible for them keeping their rooms clean and tidy, making their beds and coming home for dinner on time.

Now a part of me knew this was not fair. My sisters made all kinds of messes and I was going to pay for them. That pretty much sums up what happened for the next few years. I did get punished for their mishaps, their forgetfulness, their rebelliousness and they're "just being kids". I became more anxious about what they did and didn't do. I would strongly urge them to "clean up and smarten up," whatever it took. The "little mother" in me was being formed. Not an uncommon role in these kinds of dysfunctional families.

There were other duties that I had to become proficient in at a young age. I learned how to iron my father's shirts, to read recipes, to cook major meals and/or at least be able to answer specific questions regarding the preparation of each dish.

Mother made me nervous because I was so afraid of her I could barely read anything. I would get things all mixed up and the letters and signs and symbols in recipes would get all jumbled up to me. I stood like a little soldier trying to follow everything she was teaching me from baking to pickling, to dainties to Christmas dinners and the "perfect gravy." Although I eventually did learn a lot from my mother, to this day I still tend to recoil slightly at recipes that involve more than three steps. I have learned to cook intuitively. It works just fine.

My anxiety at making a mistake was continuous and I felt the stress and pressure to avoid verbal assault and physical punishment on a daily basis. One time, I just couldn't follow her directions and her punishment was to stand me on a stool in front of my family, put a bag on my head and call me names, telling my family how stupid I was that day. I recall my father being there and he didn't stop her on this one. I needed him to protect me. I could not protect myself from her.

Shirlee taught me that it was important to always offer help to her and others. My manners were impeccable and company would comment on what nice, well-behaved children we were, "so thoughtful!" I learned ways to please her.

One day, I decided to really please my mother. Shirlee had been away visiting her own mother for several days and was due home the following day. Jeannie, our babysitter, was looking after us. Dad was not living consistently at home as he was not in one of his periods of sobriety, but seemed to be around "somewhere."

We had a large kitchen that had green-and-white-tiled flooring. I decided to wash the floor and took some cleaning fluid out. I wasn't sure what I was using but it had a strong smell and I knew it would work. The floor began to look exceptionally clean, so clean it even began to change colour. The green was disappearing.

I was undaunted. I needed to also polish the floor with the large polisher which I could practically drive across the floor as it was almost the size of me. I vigorously carried on with the polishing process all the while noticing that not only was the green tile colour almost completely gone, but the shape of the tiles was changing too. The edges were all curling up, every single one of them. I had no idea that I had used an entire bottle of bleach to wash the floors. By the next day the polished kitchen floor tiles were rather grim looking. You couldn't walk on the floor without practically cutting your feet. My siblings were complaining.

We heard mother's car arrive. Then her car door shut and the house door opened. I felt very nervous as it was obvious something was wrong with the floor. The babysitter realized the importance of the moment and quickly pointed out to Shirlee how hard I had worked for hours on the floor, "to make you happy, Mrs. Halcrow."

With an instant of insight, seemingly invoked by the angels themselves, Mother, with a deep breath and pale, stony face, brought forward all the grace she could muster. She thanked me for my work and told me how happy she was with the floor.

I wasn't punished. Instead, my father was summoned, likely from the local legion. He appeared to have been on a real bender. He was given the task of stripping , re-tarring and retiling the floor. It was a big job. I recall his sweaty brow as he muttered religious names and undertook this penance with resignation, while my mother stood by and sipped on her rye and water. I felt sorry for him.

My training and sense of responsibility continued on. In all of this I was also developing my strength in staying calm and being able to figure things out, knowing what to do in a crisis and generally taking things in hand when either parent was not functioning or not present, which would become more frequent.

The Power of Encouragement

My Dad could be really fun with us when he was at home and Mother was gone visiting her family. At night he would tell us thrilling ghost stories that would scare and entertain us. He would joke and play shadow puppets on our walls. He would feed us apple pie, chocolates and cake for our main meals. He would take us out of town and we'd slide down sandy hills on our butts and get filthy dirty. When he got drunk he wasn't mean to us, he was only embarrassing when he fell outside in the yard and swore loudly. It was still a welcome respite.

Dad told me one day, "Barb, you can do anything. You're a really smart girl and if you want to be an astronaut, you can do that too." I wasn't sure about the astronaut part, but Dad's words were kind and inspirational. His few encouraging messages to me in my childhood stood out in direct contrast to the daily verbal attacks from my mother, "you're an evil bitch; you're nothing but a piece of garbage." I somehow knew those words weren't true, but they still affected me coming from a person I loved.

I tucked Dad's encouragement away inside, as if to protect it. It wasn't much but someone believed in me and it helped me just a little bit more to believe in myself.

Dad was also instrumental in making me literally get back on a horse that sent me sailing though the air and crashing down on a hard dirt road when I visited the Penticton Indian Band reserve with him. I was sore from head to toe. Even through my tears he wouldn't take "no" for an answer. He ordered me back on that huge animal until I learned how to manage the horse properly. Being a little person was not helpful but my father told me this was "a lesson in life" so I had to learn it. I was glad I did in the end because I ended up getting bucked off several more times and every time it happened I got more determined to get back on and complete the ride.

The Mask of Denial

As I entered my elementary school years, things at home continued on their disastrous spiral downward. The arguments between my parents became even more physically violent with the flying objects and attacks with the wooden spoons and belts, as well as knife appearances. Friends who heard Mother screaming from the street, before they knocked on our door, soon stayed clear of our home. No one seemed in control of anything.

I pretended that every day was "fine" when I hung out with my friends. There was a "code of silence" demanded by my mother. Being as our father was a well-known lawyer it was expected that we keep up appearances in spite of the family breakdown.

Becoming as strong and independent as possible was always my intention. From an early age I felt I wanted to cultivate my strength and endurance in all ways possible for my own survival and success. I also didn't want anyone to think I was "weak" and be able to take advantage of me. "Show no fear" was something I would think about often and continue to demand of myself no matter what the circumstances. This attitude of focus and determination also became an acquired skill. I believed it made me stronger when I needed my courage to keep moving myself forward. It also made it harder for me, later on, to get through to other feelings underneath my shield.

The Athlete Emerges

During this time in my first seven years of school, besides being noticed for my artistic and musical abilities, I discovered something else quite wonderful about myself. I could outrun all the girls as well as many of the boys. I could throw farther, hit baseballs better and jump higher. Everyone wanted me on their team. I won races continually and became a little school star.

In other areas I was afraid of being seen. I would hide behind the school pillars outside if I knew a teacher was around who was supervising the play area. My grades started to improve though, in spite of my fears and shyness, as I developed more self-esteem from sports. I started to get myself continually on the scholastic honour roll by using the visualization I'd developed earlier in my life to remember information and score excellent test marks in school. This visual ability began to serve me well in sports too. I would always imagine myself the winner, crossing the finish line with the kids in the crowd cheering. It felt fantastic. That part of my life seemed to be developing well for me.

The Second House

When I was thirteen years old, my parents decided to move up in the world and they sold our home. They bought property on a bank overlooking the city. The day we moved in with those countless boxes and mayhem would be the day my father suddenly disappeared again. My mother and the four of us felt confused and abandoned.

I loved my Dad and I felt a lot of grief when he left this time. He had been able to stay sober for a short while in Alcoholics Anonymous just before we moved. I had felt proud of him when he was sober. I saw he was a handsome, robust man and an accomplished lawyer. He always talked about his legal cases with me and I found his stories really interesting. I learned later that students studied his work at UBC. As children we had been hopeful that maybe things would eventually work out between our parents since our mother too had joined him for a time in sobriety. At this point though, we really wondered what was going to happen to us all.

The Importance of Allies

It makes a difference for all of us to have someone in our corner who sees, understands and accepts us even if we cannot accept or know ourselves. It helps with the sense of isolation that kids feel when they're caught in their parents' illness and abuse and when other people shun them. It made a difference for me.

My Brother

My allies came in several ways. Within my family I was close for periods of time to my older brother, Rob, even though he chose to take off from the house with his friends whenever he had the chance. Being the eldest boy-child he didn't have the same responsibilities as I did. He had hunting and fishing to learn from Dad, things that I knew also pressured him to be "a man."

Since Rob and I were close in age and looked very much alike with our darker hair and colouring, many people thought we were twins. We liked that. I got to learn how to fish with Rob and my Dad when we travelled around the province. It got unnerving at times when Dad would drive drunk and crash the Jeep into mountainsides, but Rob and I hung in there and coped well together.

Rob was caring and protective toward me, especially in his later years as a teen and young adult. He had a wonderful sensitivity and gentleness about him. I truly adored him. I believe he was a natural healer too. He grew to be a tall man at six feet two inches. Later on in my mid-teens, he would step in between Mom and me when she would physically launch herself at me in her rages.

Second Sister

The other ally I felt was in my corner was my sister Lindsay. She was two years younger than me and she would sit in the school stands when I'd run my races or watch me play field hockey or basketball and scream my name out in support. Most of the time I could hear her voice above all others. Lindsay had her own problems and her sense of survival as a middle child was at stake, but she was caring and steadfast in her presence for me. She knew a lot of what was going on in my life on a daily basis. In fact, she was the only one who really did know as she ended up sharing some of the very same traumas.

Aunts and Uncles

My father's sisters and brothers were also in my corner but more sporadically. They would visit and check in when they could. They knew that their brother Gordon had a serious alcohol problem and there were marital issues, but they really didn't know the extent of the chaos and violence. They were respectful and loving and didn't want to interfere in our lives. I found out years later that my Dad's eldest brother, Jim, had considered adopting me. In retrospect it was probably best I stayed where I was. It would have been hard for me to leave my brother and sisters.

Teachers

Some teachers at school also took an interest in me. They tried to be allies, especially my sports coaches, but I kept more emotionally distant from them because adults generally scared me.

One of the Guidance Counsellors at my junior secondary school called me into her office one day to have a chat about "what was really going on at home." I flatly denied everything. I had myself believing by then that it was not that unusual for the eldest girl to be responsible for running the house, sewing my sisters' clothes and working part-time to make ends meet. Being on welfare for several years at that point was an embarrassing challenge and sometimes the cupboards got pretty bare. The school counsellor indicated to me she knew things were hard between my mother and me. I never told her anything that I knew would get me into serious trouble. I was afraid to trust the counsellor with what would be considered be a betrayal of family secrets.

My Connection with Spirit

Early in my teen years I began to leave the house for longer and longer periods of time. I would sit in the neighbourhood tree house or hike long miles out to the local hills. I would be gone for hours on end.

I found in nature a great solace and a sense of spirit that calmed and soothed me. With my natural sensitivity I believe this solitude in nature increased my intuition and contributed to my ability to listen to my inner guidance.

I prayed a lot too. I had my favourite spots with special trees and rocks where I would go and talk to God. I loved those trees; they felt like kind, older spirit beings. I would pray to God to help me and help my family. I believed God could hear me. I believed in something more because I could feel it. I could feel something happen to me when I prayed. Something would change inside me. I felt better and stronger. I always thought about angels too, because when I was a little girl I believed I saw them and I believed they were still around.

I had learned about prayer in our United Church Sunday School. I found Sunday School too boring and I rarely wanted to go, but both parents were firm on this ritual. The whole "Son of God/ Holy Spirit" stuff confused me. I did like some of the singing though because it was joyful. I also enjoyed the stories of Jesus because he felt like a real person to me with the messages about love. I would dream about him often. I felt he was my friend.

When I was about eleven years old I read "Corinthians 1:13" from the Holy Bible. I learned it in the United Church Sunday School. I felt the part that described the attributes of Love really resonated with me. I began to read it every day. I felt something deeper being stirred up in me. I was by nature a very loving child who really cared about people, but the hellish alcoholism, violence and severe depression of my mother were almost all-consuming. I needed to read something that inspired my soul and spirit.

It felt very good to read this passage:

"Love is patient, Love is Kind. It does not envy, It does not boast, it is not proud. It is not rude, it is not self-seeking. It is not easily angered. It keeps no record of wrongs. Love does not delight in evil, but rejoices in the truth. It always protects, always trusts, always hopes, always perseveres. Love never fails."
(connect.in.com 2010)

There were two lines in this passage that struck my heart and mind. "*It keeps no record of wrongs*" and "*Love never fails*". I completely believed those words because I could feel them. They felt powerful and transforming to me. I didn't quite know what it was all about but every time I read those words, I felt more compassionate, happier and stronger inside. I wanted to be strong. I knew this statement about love was my truth.

Alateen

When I was 13 years old my brother Rob and I started Alateen in Penticton with a couple of other teens. Alateen is a part of Al-Anon which helps teens cope with parents who abuse alcohol. My parents, in one of their periods of sobriety, had introduced us to a fellow AA member and his teenage sons. As teenagers, we all agreed to start this venture.

I learned about "Higher Power" and added that to my spiritual understanding. It was a good experience for Rob and me. It helped us because it meant that we could share experiences with other kids who had alcoholic parents and not feel so isolated and helpless. "Let go and let God," they'd always say. A part of The Serenity Prayer that was adopted by Alcoholics Anonymous and Al-Anon became imbued in my mind and I repeated it often throughout my life:

"God grant me the serenity to accept the things I cannot change. Courage to change the things I can, and wisdom to know the difference."
(Niebuhr, 1934)

This hard learning of acceptance, change and letting go would become a life long struggle in practice for me. It would take a long time for me to sift through myriad experiences and gain the strength to understand what "letting go" really meant. Ultimately, I was going to have to learn how to respectfully allow people to live their own lives and make their own mistakes without my interference, no matter how frightened and uncomfortable I would feel.

My spiritual journey would alter and shift over the years to follow, and I would explore countless churches and spiritual expressions until I would eventually come to my own simple, non-religious spiritual understanding.

Fighting Back

When I hit the age of fourteen something happened. Maybe it was the involvement in the Alateen group that helped and likely a few hormones too. I started to show my anger. I was fed up with being so emotionally and physically targeted, disrespected and violated by my mother. I was getting stronger and I began to verbally confront her. My verbal confrontations contributed to immediate violent escalations on her part.

She would lose control and come at me with more vengeance—one time with a knife tucked under a towel. I froze in fear while my brother grabbed her arm. It was as if once I started to open my mouth, I couldn't be stopped. I had to tell her how I felt and that she had no right to treat me so badly. It began to pour out of me as I started to yell and shout at her for the first time in my life. I was standing up to her and I couldn't be silenced.

Both Lindsay and Rob were constantly getting in between Mother and me in their efforts to prevent me from being physically injured. I would not allow myself to fight back or strike her physically. I couldn't; it was not part of the moral/ethical deal I made with myself. I was also aware that I could possibly really hurt her if I did and I could not live with that.

There was lots of fist-pummelling, hair-grabbing and dragging me around on her part, but I kept up my verbal confrontation for several months until I managed to get a hold of myself.

The Old "Tea in the Bottle" Trick

I also began to do things that Alateen teaches you not to do—like throw out your parents' alcohol. Well, I didn't quite do that, but I replaced my mother's full 26'er of rye with tea. I found it was a perfect match in colour. I watched her sip it, look at the bottle, then leave the house. She returned several minutes later with the "we are not amused" look on her face. She had taken the bottle down the government liquor store and complained about a "bad bottle." She told me all the guys tested it and began to laugh loudly telling her it was tea.

She demanded I replace the alcohol. Well, luckily for me I had poured it all into a bowl. I really didn't want to die so young. I told my brother and sisters what I had done. They were horrified I'd be so bold. Then we all laughed ourselves silly.

"Pass the Humour, Please!"

Humour continues to be important in my life. As a child I knew members of my father's Scottish clan best and there were always lots of fast-paced jokes and humorous stories whenever they came around.

As children huddled together on our own little life raft, we seemed to hit a time when our humour was becoming well developed—thanks to the "material" we had to work with! We'd make fun of Mom's expressions. When she drank we noticed she'd acquire a distinct English accent. Out would come all kinds of British expressions. These expressions were red flags, signs that she was on the turn toward more intoxication; but we had to cope and humour was a good way to do it. Sometimes we'd all just adopt our own English accents right along with her to get her to laugh at herself. Sometimes it worked—and we sounded like a bunch of crazed babbling fools—and sometimes it didn't.

During this time I also began to direct my younger sisters not to pick Mom up if she collapsed on the floor in her inebriation. "Just let her lie there," I'd say, "We're not her servants." So she did lie there for hours on end calling repeatedly to be taken to her room.

There were other incidents during this time frame. But suffice it to say this was a significant turning point for me and in my relationship with my mother. It felt good to assert myself even if I got more bruising. I was taking some of my power back and she was aware of it. I was now moving from the role of family "scapegoat" to the family "hero."

Another Decision

When I arrived in tenth grade at sixteen years of age, I made another decision. I decided I would win the Junior

Secondary School's top "Female Athlete of the Year Award." I felt I could do it. I had proven myself to be a strong athlete but there were other strong girls who were equally talented. I felt my competition was formidable. I felt passionate about this quest and I vowed to keep my mantra alive; I repeated to myself daily, "I can do it!"

I didn't want the award for me directly; I initially wanted it to clear my family name. I was tired of the shame, humiliation and degradation that came from the impact of my parents' illnesses and behaviour. I didn't want it connected to me any longer. My name as a "Halcrow" had to be redeemed and respected and I felt it was up to me to do it.

I continuously visualized myself winning the award. I wanted it badly. I told myself I would not be defeated. I ran for miles on my own after school as part of my coping and part of my training. And I prayed. I never told anyone how badly I wanted this award.

Finally the big day came. "And the Female Athlete of the Year goes to: Barbara Halcrow."

Yes, I did it.

The Counsellor Appears

As children, we always knew our mother was "not well." We knew that she was decisively different—odd in her thoughts and expressions, and outrageous and frightening in her behaviour. In her hallucinations she thought she saw the devil and would smash glasses and plates at the walls. It went on for years and it was very disturbing.

Her near-death suicide attempts with pills and alcohol that sent her into the Penticton Emergency Department and then into the Psychiatric Unit were also very distressing. She was given medication that she would hide in her cheek and spit out.

One of her attempts at suicide was more unusual when she attempted to drown herself. She came home very intoxicated one evening and was dripping wet from head to toe with bits of sand all over her. She had immersed herself in Penticton's Skaha Lake. She tearfully told us, as she stood in the doorway, that she wanted to die.

Our father, sitting on the sofa, had dropped in a few days earlier in his last cameo appearance at home. Gordon scoffed and made fun of her wet clothes. I was surprised at his reaction and in that moment my heart saw my mother with tenderness. Her action was such an obvious cry for help, comfort and attention. She seemed totally lost. I began to view my mother with a far more open, compassionate heart.

"Out of the depths of our despair we build our character."

I don't know where this phrase came from and Mom would read this phrase often to me, then cry deeply in her own despair and depression. It stuck with me. Though Mom frightened me with her violent outbursts, she really began to sadden me more. I saw her acute suffering for all the losses in her life, for her longing to be understood, accepted and loved. She was a lonely woman and I felt great empathy toward her.

I began to ask Mom many questions about her life to try to understand her. She began to open and respond.

I sat up with her for long hours, just listening carefully to her. I was seeing her more objectively with sincere curiosity to find out what had happened to her. How did she become so ill? Was she abused in her life?

She relayed to me how she threw a knife at one of her sisters when she was nine years old, narrowly missing her. She didn't know why she did it except that she was angry at the time and felt her sister was too competitive with her. She said she could not recall being physically or sexually abused by anyone. She only could say that it was expected of her to be "a perfect lady."

Mom told me she never got over losing the love of her life, her fiancée, Max, who was blown to bits in the war. She ruminated on this grief and would tell me many times how she would walk the streets of Vancouver when he died, looking for him in her sorrow, and that when she met my father, her own Dad did not want her to marry him because Gordon drank too much. She talked about many things regarding her life and her longing for her own father to love her. She told me how protective he was of her, but how she never really heard him tell her he loved her, until he was on his death bed.

The counsellor in me continued to develop.

At one point my youngest sister, who spent most of her time with friends away from home as a way of coping, had to leave our home. Child Protection Services intervened as she was showing significant signs of emotional distress at school. It was hard for me to see my sister leave but I was relieved for her too.

Mother was devastated by losing her youngest child. Her acute mental instability and our family's secrets were being further exposed. It was also clear we would all be leaving her one by one in some fashion or another.

There was a part of me that wanted to "save" her as I constantly feared her complete demise and ultimate death. However, in time, I would also have to learn to let her go and accept her life path as it was.

"This One's for Me!"

When I reached the twelfth grade, I was seventeen years old. I made another decision. I wanted once again to be the "Female Athlete of the Year." This time, this award would be solely for me.

I set about to do what I did before. I told myself, "I can do it!" and I visualized my success. Again, my competition was excellent. I continued on as usual, joining all the teams I was interested in like track and field, basketball, field hockey and distance running.

Track and field was my love but it was also quite nerve-wracking. There is something to be said about the moment when you are sitting in the starting blocks waiting for the gun to go off so you can tear up the turf in the 100-, 200- or 400-metre race. The incredible amount of nervous energy that is pouring through your body as you are poised, holding back, legs shaking, waiting. Those long seconds. These moments and all the training, leading up to the second the gun is fired, take great discipline and laser focus. This focus and discipline translated into other areas of my life.

Once I got going out of the starting blocks, I psychologically had to read my competition and pace myself accordingly. In a small town you get to know all the other athletes and their strengths. I was particularly good at the 200 and 400 metres. I figured I had the edge on most of my competitors with my strength and endurance. I broke the Okanagan Valley record in the Regional Track and Field finals in the 200 metres that spring. I was pleased.

I hit a snag though with regard to basketball in this year of high school. I couldn't seem to get through my "stage fright" when it came to playing for the Senior A girls basketball team. My shyness, my self-consciousness and my fear of "being seen" or making a mistake came haunting me from my home life. Sometimes, I would freeze up under pressure and I wouldn't play as well.

I didn't get picked for the A team that year and I was crestfallen. I felt my chances for the award were dashed. However, suddenly along came another teacher, who heard about some of us not making the A team and he decided he wanted to coach girls basketball. As we grouped together that day to form a new team, the atmosphere became far more relaxed for me. The coach was caring and personally supportive. I completely excelled with this group and we surprised everyone by winning our division title.

Later on in the school awards ceremony, I would learn my fate. Did I get the Female Athlete of the Year Award? Yes, I did, and I was even surprised that I had succeeded in amassing the most points ever as a female athlete at the time. I also received a "Citizenship Award" for Student Council/Community service.

I had proven to myself that, no matter what was going on at home, no matter what my parents were or were not doing, I had made a decision to succeed. I had put in the extra work and continued to believe in my mantra, "I can do it!" Things were beginning to fall into place.

I now had my sights on attending the University of Victoria, where my brother was. I decided that I really wanted to be a Physical Education Teacher and Guidance Counsellor.

Black Widow Haunting

There's nothing like a good spider scare, some would say, except in my case it was a bit more than that. It started when I was about to go off to university. That one hot summer there was an infestation of black widow spiders all over the grassy bank where our home was located. There had to be a concerted bank burn and pine tree cutting by all the neighbours to deal with them.

My room was in the basement and the bedroom window screen had been slightly torn over time. They were big, those black widow spiders. You could plainly see the red hour glasses on their abdomens, as they liked to hang upside down in their webs, protecting their large egg sacks and waiting for unsuspecting prey to land. I saw them everywhere when I was outside tending to the garden and yard work; then I saw them crawling up inside our stairs. I knew they were poisonous so I took my RAID can and killed them every chance I got. I hated doing it, because it was scary to be around them, but it felt safer than feeling constantly under siege.

I soon realized some of them were coming into my bedroom through the screen and as soon as one was in, others followed quickly. One got into the top of my closet and hung there menacingly for days and I couldn't get her out easily. It was scary.

One afternoon I was passing through a doorway when I was enveloped by a web. I had studied the black widow's nesting patterns out of my terror fascination and noticed they were not the normal patterns of other spiders. The webs appeared tangled and in disarray. I had walked into one that had been formed completely across the basement hallway door. I knew in an instant that a black widow spider was nearby, but it was darker in the basement and I couldn't see my surroundings very well. I felt terrified. I knew the spider could be anywhere.

I slowly stepped back in through the tangled web again and saw it below my left leg on the door. It truly was the biggest black widow I'd ever laid eyes on. Of course, I felt it was just waiting for me.

"No!" I screamed inside and from my near frozen stance this spider too, saw its demise.

It seemed these creatures were drawn to me. I could feel them instinctively whenever there was one around, not just the black widows but any spider now. Except one particular time.

It was a Saturday morning and I was still sleeping. I heard my sister Lindsay's voice somewhere shouting, "Barbara, wake up! Wake up!!"

As I opened my eyes I saw it. The large black widow spider was directly above my head, dangling down quickly. She was about to land on me when I was able to move my head to the side and leap out of the way. The widow immediately touched down to the pillow where I'd just been. I was in complete shock for a second with my heart pounding through my chest, trying not to think of the inevitable. I took a book and smashed the spider.

From that moment on, I was not the same. This incident would traumatize me for over thirty years. Family, friends and lovers would see the aftermath of this event manifesting during my sleep. I would suddenly bolt up in a panic state, eyes wide open, heart pounding, then dive out of bed, insisting there was a spider coming down to land on me. My nightmares would be filled with them as they seemed to become representative of all that terrified me.

In my waking reality I would freeze and be unable to speak or barely breathe if one of these creatures appeared. I had to do something.

Facing My Fears

How does one get over that kind of trauma? The same way I had done with my other fears. I had to face it down. I was determined that I was not going to be so disempowered and controlled by such tiny creatures.

In facing this phobia I decided to study them as I'd observed and studied other aspects of nature. I forced myself to do this by looking at pictures of them and reading about them bit by bit. It was a hard, terrifying task.

As I continued to learn about spiders in general I observed them differently. I saw how they communicated, fought with each other and protected their nests. I saw and felt how there was an intelligence within them that desired to live, to just be. They meant no harm.

Facing this fear though was not a short venture to be sure. However, as I delved down into my emotional self I realized the black widow spider was a female energy, and she was also connected psychologically to the female energy of my mother. The kind of trauma that my mother had impacted on me was not dissimilar in some ways as to my perception of what the black widows had done. It was all about feeling trapped, violated and terrorized. This exploration took me years to uncover and come to terms with. I would be faced with spider nightmares many times over. But there seemed to be something even more than what I had uncovered.

Power Animals

Further insights would arrive. I stopped into an Aboriginal shop in Hope, BC, one day. As I entered the shop, the First Nations woman at the counter kindly greeted me and then promptly stated, "Oh, I see one of your power animals is a spider!" Well, this was not information I wanted to hear! I practically stopped breathing but I was curious to pursue this area with her.

She said she saw my connection and that I was not using my creativity enough. The spider is known to have an intelligent, creative energy. She went on to explain other facets of our "power animals" and how we often fear our power animals and draw them to us until we understand the teachings. I knew a few things about "drawing in our fears" at that point! She further explained that the spider, with its eight legs representing infinity and the weaving of its web, is not dissimilar to humanity's own weavings in the complexity and spirituality in the creation of our lives.

I left her store with thoughtfulness. I explored this area some more.

Several years went by and I found myself sitting in an

interview for a job I wasn't sure would be right for me. I was asked a question and just before I answered my eyes were drawn to the window nearby. I saw a spider come out for a moment on its web. At that moment I knew I would not want this job. I knew that the spider was warning me about becoming entangled in this position, that it would rob me of my energy.

This new perception had come as part of my own healing. The spider warnings would continue to unfold in other situations and in some of my personal relationships. I really began to take notice and the spider symbols would all prove to be true.

I'll be honest, I still don't like some spiders, but I do respect them as part of life and have attended to the warnings they have given to me in my dream and waking state. This fear, without question, was worth facing.

Sexual Abuse

For me, sexuality was fascinating, confusing and violating before it ever felt completely comfortable. That experience unfortunately may be more common than not for others as well.

As a child growing up I heard and saw things that were not healthy and not meant for young ones. I knew both of my parents had affairs. They conversed and fought about them openly, especially when my father was around. There was also open conflict regarding these affairs with other men and woman who came to the house in intoxication and anger.

When my father finally left our home permanently my

mother wanted to get on with her life as well. She was still a very attractive woman who was lonely, and she wanted to be with someone. She still dressed well and indeed still had her movie-star looks.

Unfortunately for us, her male suitors became numerous. On one occasion my mother was upset and revealed to me she had been sexually assaulted by a man she had met at a bar. I felt upset but somehow oddly calm as I experienced her distress. I ended up consoling and counselling her for several hours for her to know it "wasn't her fault."

Before I left for university, several men lived with us for a few months, and one even had two nine- and ten-year-old "demon boys" who ran us ragged. Their father, Dean, was a brash, know-it-all, red-necked man who announced he was going to marry our mother and that was that. We were not pleased.

After he abused my mother physically, we banded together and confronted him. We demanded that Mother get rid of him. "Dean and the demons" were shown the door.

What became confusing, disturbing and eventually traumatizing was how Mother began to deteriorate when her breakups with men would occur. She drank even more in her loneliness. She would reminisce in her depth of grief when she drank while the smooth voice of Nat King Cole played in the background.

Things also began to change in another way that would unsettle and distress me further.

In my late teens, when I would be putting on my makeup to go out with my boyfriends, I noticed my mother began to stare at me. She would make comments that didn't feel right to me. I felt her look at me with a degree of sexual attraction. She would also become very intoxicated and wanted to be affectionate and caress me. Although part of me understood her loneliness and need for affection, I felt I was being violated. When I pushed her hands away, her touch would turn violent with hair-pulling or hitting and screaming as my rejection would be too much for her. There would be more sleepless nights to contend with.

Mom molested me once by fondling my breasts in front of a female friend of mine and it completely stunned me. It happened very fast. I was very disturbed about it in addition to it also being a sexual public violation. I tried to push it out of my mind. I wanted to keep it away from myself but I ended up having nightmares to remind me it happened. Years later I would have to face these violations in therapy along with the rest of the abuse. I would have to acknowledge myself as an incest survivor.

The Nest Empties

I finally left home and entered the University of Victoria; I was ready to enter my next life phase. My brother, Rob, was at university there and my sister, Catherine, had also moved to Victoria. That left my sister, Lindsay, at home alone with Mom.

Only a few weeks after my entry to university, Lindsay wrote to let Rob and me know she had spent several nights locked in the bathroom, as Mom was physically violating her in various ways. Mom was also repeatedly stabbing the bathroom door with a butcher knife trying to get in.

Rob and I flew home and supported Lindsay in speaking with child protection services. Lindsay was immediately moved to what amounted to a rundown men's single-room-occupancy hotel, as there wasn't anything else for her. It was not the safest place, but it was better than being at home.

At this point with our mother's loss of us all, we became very concerned that she would choose to end her life. She did not, though she was unsuccessful in one more suicide attempt involving pills and alcohol. She was sent to an alcohol and drug and treatment centre in Victoria for six weeks. Although she gained her sobriety for a period of time, she would not open herself to the confrontational style of the counselling program. She eventually returned home to the same situation and began drinking and dating again.

My Brother's Return to Spirit

My brother and I had a special bond of love that we both recognized from our earlier years growing up together. It felt deep, pure and gentle.

He was a good student, a strong athlete and liked by all who met him. His tall, well-toned physique and dark, good looks made him stand out. He belonged to the rowing club at the University of Victoria and he was fun and supportive. He graduated from the University of Victoria.

On June 7, Rob, Lindsay, Mom and I were all at Mom's home in Penticton. Rob was about to leave that afternoon on a hitchhiking trip to Europe. His plan was to travel for two months and then return and head up to Prince George to teach Geography.

That same morning at about 11:00 a.m. my father suddenly pulled up in a white cab. He looked dirty, dishevelled and beardy. As I looked out the door window and saw him come toward the house, I said to my sister Lindsay, "Remember this moment, it is very significant!"

Dad entered and no one was pleased to see him this way. "I don't know why I'm here," he said. "I've been working up on the railway lines and something just told me to come."

Rob continued to pack his knapsack with some distress regarding his father's appearance. It had been a very strained relationship between them with Dad's alcoholism and intermittent bullying of Rob in his early years. It was obvious now that Dad was going to be coming in the car with us when we took Rob out to the highway toward Kelowna. There, he'd meet up with few friends before travelling about and eventually flying off to England.

We let Rob out with his knapsack, hugged him and said our goodbyes. I had a terrible feeling when I hugged him that I would never see him again.

On June 17, ten days later, two RCMP arrived at Mom's door to tell us Rob had been killed in a motor vehicle accident near Hereford, England. He'd been hitchhiking and a tire had blown in the van that had picked him up. The van had crashed, killing three people.

The death of a loved one, especially when a child predeceases their parents, brings its own unique and terrible experience. It can lead to profound grief as well as profound growth.

My mother was immediately emotionally shattered. I

stayed in control and spoke to the police. I stayed in control for many days to come to ensure everything was managed. My father's family came and went and gave their support as they could.

For various reasons, not fully explained or understood to this day, Rob's body was never brought home to us. He was buried at Hereford Cathedral, England.

Rob had been a Boy Scout. With the coordinating efforts of some of our kinfolk in Britain, along with the involvement of the International Boy Scouts Association, they gave him a full, honouring funeral. His body remains there. His friends from the Penticton Senior High School also honoured him for many years with the Robert Halcrow Award for Best All Round Student.

This was a hard situation for me in not being able to fully say goodbye to Rob for a long time. I've had to accept and forgive things as they were. Perhaps it would have been too much for me, or any of us, to bear if he had been brought home and if I'd seen his body. I'll never know. There was a memorial service, which was a blur to me.

My father found out about Rob's death from a fellow friend who happened to see it in the local paper. By this time Dad was down on "skid row" in Downtown Eastside, Vancouver. If he had not been spiritually directed to come down to Penticton that day on June 7, he would never have been able to see his son before Rob's untimely death. Spirit indeed works in mysterious ways.

With the death of my brother I felt I was the only one left at the head of our family unit whom I could really rely on. In reality it wasn't so different than before. I accepted that thought. I had to keep trusting in myself, my intuition and my spirit and I had to keep going forward as before, never giving up. I wanted to graduate from university, be successful, be able to support myself and eventually get married. I wasn't too sure how it was all going to turn out, but I was determined to find a way, even though I could not see anything too clearly at that point in my life.

Career Beginnings

I worked part-time jobs and continued to attend UVIC summer school. I successfully graduated from the University of Victoria as planned. I became a Social Worker and worked in various communities in southern BC, and I eventually made my way to Vancouver. It was difficult, challenging work, but I had a good aptitude for it and certainly good background experiences, while being "trained on the job" growing up.

My Father Goes to "Jail"

During the next several years after my brother's death, I knew my father was around in different areas in greater Vancouver, cycling between sobriety and relapse. I was twenty-five and working for the Ministry of Human Resources as a Social Worker in Chilliwack. I got a call from one of my aunts urging me to "do something about your father!"

Gordon was in trouble. I was to find out from his lawyer that he had been charged with defrauding a Vancouver Branch of the Ministry of Human Resources, the very organization I worked for. I was shocked and angered that this situation had again fallen on me to deal with my parent in this way. I didn't feel I had the strength to walk away from family pressure and my sense of being responsible to deal with Dad—not quite yet.

I resentfully met with his lawyer, Jim, who took me aside in the courthouse to lay it out.

"Look, Barbara, your Dad is very well known in this province and we'd really like to keep this whole thing out of the papers, as it doesn't do our profession any good. Make sure he stays sober, has a better suit on and is back in here tomorrow for court proceedings."

"Keep my father sober? Are you kidding me?" Well, I knew I had my work cut out for me. I had no place to put him overnight where he would agree to go. I didn't know parts of Vancouver very well at the time. Dad spotted a local hotel I'd not seen before and suggested it would be fine. I really didn't like the look of it and didn't want to go in, but he really insisted, saying he knew the manager and we could get a good deal. I wasn't sure if that was a good thing or not.

"OK," I thought, "just this one time only, to keep him straight and get him into the courtroom." He asked for the "best room."

I met a large cockroach that evening prancing across the floor. "Well, would you look at that, Dad!" I realized later I was in the Cobalt Hotel, a well-known establishment of disrepute in Vancouver's Downtown Eastside; it was not exactly your crème de la crème.

As in years gone by, that evening Dad began to tell stories mostly about the war years while I kept watch for small friends scurrying by. We shared some red wine he'd brought in. He didn't leave the hotel that night. I chalked it all up as "just another experience" in my life.

We made it to the courtroom the next morning and Gordon was given a slap on the wrist with a suspended sentence by the judge. He was ordered to serve his "jail time" at the Kelowna Seniors Retirement Home. The judge's message was one more altercation with the law and my Dad would be incarcerated. I knew he'd really lucked out and part of me wished he'd paid his dues for theft like anyone else. In a way, though, he'd already been paying for them with some of his own significant losses, loneliness and the shame that the addiction brought him.

He managed to stay in Kelowna for about three months before getting evicted for his disorderly conduct. The same story evolved in his transfer elsewhere until he finally ended up in Shaughnessy Hospital in Vancouver. He'd been hospitalized with a bout of malaria from his earlier days in WW II when he'd flown into the Burma Jungle.

A Social Worker called me up one day. She said she felt she had a place for Dad that he would really fit into. It was George Derby Centre, a Veteran's Retirement complex in Burnaby, BC. The Social Worker felt he needed to be with men and women of military rank who understood the war years. Although I was not eager for another venture with Dad, the transfer was made and he quickly responded well to this change. He flourished there with a regained sense of self-respect he had not had for many years. At George Derby, he'd found a place of acceptance belonging in this special community. I was glad for him. It was a remarkable personal transformation from Vancouver's skid row in the

Downtown Eastside to his new home.

Gordon fared very well at George Derby for the rest of his days. His military position was reflected back to him, from other ranked men and woman, in ways that he respected. He became President of the Residence Council and made valuable contributions. He did much better than my mother in the end.

He began to send me birthday and Christmas cards and told me, "I'm proud of you!" I really appreciated it.

My career path was shifting then and I decided to go overseas and teach English as a Second Language in Seoul, Korea in 1997. While I was in Korea I had a premonition that my father would die soon. I began to write him a long, heartfelt letter. It was my second one. I wrote him years earlier to tell him of his impact on my life, the alcoholism and his abandonment of our family. Though he got the first letter from me he did not say a word about it. This time though, I had an urgent sense to tell him of the good things that I knew about him and of his earlier accomplishments as a respected lawyer. I wanted him to know how much fun he was at times when we were children. Most of all I wanted to tell him that I loved him.

I left the letter in an envelope sitting on a table in my apartment in Korea for several days before sending it. I was aware I was procrastinating.

Dad died suddenly at age seventy-four, two days before he would have received my letter. My inner guidance had been right in urging me to write him. I was saddened at his death and disappointed in myself. He deserved to hear from me before he passed on. I clearly saw that there was an opportunity for me to give more love, appreciation and understanding to him. I lost that opportunity. With regret, I took the lesson in hand.

Spirituality and Sexual Identity

I was raised to be a heterosexual woman. I liked men and dated often. I wanted to get married and have children and that's all I knew. What was to happen next, however, changed everything and took me on a journey that proved to be more challenging and insightful than I could ever imagine.

In my first year of university I met a senior student in the woman's residence. I was nineteen years old and "Carol" was twenty-three. We developed a strong emotional bond. She was beautiful, loving, smart and fun. She was everything I ever wanted in anyone. We loved each other and openly stated that. We were affectionate and soon began to sleep together in her suite. We both also continued to date men without a hint of jealously between us.

Neither of us had much exposure to gay or lesbian culture. Though we discussed this aspect of our relationship, we never concluded we were anything but heterosexual and loved being with each other. Carol was kind and loving to me and I found the relationship very healing.

Our relationship just seemed so simple. I only knew I loved her and that being with her sexually was just part my own natural spiritual and physical need to express myself. We stayed together through the year until she had to leave upon her graduation.

I stayed in contact with her and we continued to meet

up between male partners. One day Carol told me she was going to marry a man in the legal profession. She explained that her family would never accept her relationship with me. I was heartbroken. I told myself I would never be with a woman again. I decided to abandon that part of myself and would never speak of it.

Shortly after, I fell in love with a kind man named David, and we became engaged to be married. However, the relationship began to falter, especially after my brother died. I became depressed from my brother's death and got involved in fundamentalist religion for a while, which forbade sex before marriage. That spiritual persuasion did not last long in my life but it did add to the dissolution of my relationship with David.

As I pursued my career I started meeting up with women in my professional circles that were forthright in their interest in me and, soon thereafter, I started to live a bisexual lifestyle. This lifestyle proved to be highly varied but very confusing for me and my female lovers.

My fear of acknowledging my own lesbianism was playing itself out. I still enjoyed and cared for men and I began to feel the pressure from some members of the women's community to accept the label "lesbian" in terms of my *total* identity. I didn't feel that being a lesbian was my complete identity and never would be. My own inner struggle continued. It was ten years of bisexual back-and-forth experiences.

It became apparent that my relationships with women were consciously provoking me to become more aware, open and honest. These relationships and my involvement in feminist politics were carving a spiritual and sexual pathway for me toward a more woman-centred reality—a reality I needed to have for my own life's development.

I began to experience a tremendous amount of fun, rapport and overall emotional and spiritual healing in my relationships with women. We knew each other's pain, strengths and vulnerabilities. We knew each other physically, emotionally and spiritually.

One day an inner light bulb went on. I realized that this deeper spiritual and emotional connection that I first experienced with Carol was the most important part of my intimate relationships I'd been looking for; this was something I'd not found with the men in my life.

There was still a problem for me in my newfound integrated identity. It nagged at me and held me back from a clear sense of myself within my relationships. It was my mother's impact.

I knew I had issues with my father too, but I felt a little clearer about those troubled areas. That pain felt more easily understood. Alcoholism and my experience with boundary violations with men were spoken about more openly.

What had happened between my mother and me in my early years; what did that infer, if anything, in terms of my sexuality with women? Maybe all this sexual activity with women was really about wanting to find my lost mother? How could I come to terms with that? How could I talk about it? I wasn't hearing anyone else talking about this kind of mother and daughter incest issue at the time. I needed help to face these issues and the deeper wounds. It felt frightening and I knew I had to get help.

Re-opening the Wounds

Through a friend I met Julie, a skilled feminist therapist in Vancouver. In my state of denial I figured I'd need about three therapy sessions to deal with my entire past, no sweat. As it turned out it, it was extremely painful and often terrifying to be in consistent therapy for almost two years. I was 29 yrs old when I began.

Julie was consciously and compassionately in the right place to help me move through a massive amount of intense, emotional material.

I began to face my abuse, grief, abandonment, as well as the meaning of my relationships with men and women. I learned how to separate what feelings were mine and what I had absorbed from my family members, especially my mother. I had to accept that I was an incest survivor.

My identity as a woman, as a loving, sexual being, began to clear more with considerable relief. I was able to understand my own development from a child into womanhood. I began to appreciate my braveness, coping skills and strengths and, I started to love myself more.

I concluded that of course I had been looking for my mother, my father and in some ways, my brother too. These were deep primary losses for me, as for anyone, losses that would take time to more fully resolve. I was able to see that I had the courage and capacity to be able to be in intimate relationships with men and women. It became clearer that the broadness of my own sexuality was a healthy natural expression, whether I had been sexually abused or not. I was really drawn toward authentic intimate relationships rather than intimate relationships based primarily on gender.

In my overall exploration of sexuality I saw how most of us are bisexual in nature and how our enculturation has immense impact on our sexual identity. I was able to appreciate how much society's homophobia affects us all and contributes to fear and confusion regarding the fullness of our capacity to love. I know things continue to change as people are courageously overcoming fear and moving forward in truth.

Owning My Anger

This was a tough area for me. Even though I was a loving person and only wanted to see myself that way, I was also angry. I had made a moral/ethical agreement with myself that I would never intentionally hurt anyone. I refused to be like either of my parents and for me to know this angry part of myself scared me.

I worried deep inside that perhaps I could do the same harm to someone else that had been done to me. I was afraid of my own rage coming out. I struggled to allow myself to talk about my hurt and anger. I had strengthened in understanding, love and compassion over the years; however, my degree of resentment and anger was still hidden in the shadow of denial.

I began to literally exercise it out as I was used to doing. I ran a lot. I threw rocks into the ocean and beat my bed up with a bat and tennis racket; I screamed into my pillow and yelled and cried when I drove my car down the highway. I'm sure I looked a bit crazy and probably was in some of those moments, but it all had to be released. I had to let myself know that I could potentially hurt someone verbally and maybe physically if I didn't own and manage this difficult past—this part of myself.

I learned anger management and applied it to my life. I took a self-defence course for women. Learning how to effectively defend myself empowered me and I felt stronger, freer and more in control of my feelings as they arose. Facing my fear to ensure I stopped the cycle of abuse was a gift to myself.

Moving On

At the age of thirty, it was time to leave my family and all the responsibilities I'd acquired growing up. I knew I had to leave to be free. All the therapy I'd gone through had also shown me that it was best to make another career change as well.

In the meantime, my mother had married her second husband, who now had to deal with her alcoholism and mental health problems. He seemed very caring of her but also unclear in who had entered his life.

My spirit took me to Winnipeg, Manitoba to start a new life with new career opportunities. In Winnipeg, I became involved in several relationships with woman and I grew more conscious in the gay community. With deeper relationships with women there also led to more heartache and learning to contend with. It was very hard and at times quite confusing. Essentially, I was still learning about relationships "on the job."

One woman, in jest, told me, "there are fifty rules in the lesbian community and you've just broken forty-nine of them!" Of course I was eager to know what the fiftieth one was! I think I found out.

I also had significant and valuable employment opportunities. I stayed in Winnipeg for nine years and grew immensely from the richness and creativity of that wonderful community of souls.

I also began my Masters Degree in Social Work as a specific scholastic challenge to myself. I wanted to advance my career and I wasn't too sure how it would all unfold. I just knew it felt right. I was quite accomplished in many areas of individual and group therapy at that point; however, I wanted to shift my direction to an area that held greater potential for professional and personal growth. My spirit nudged me forward.

Some Resolution in Death

While in Winnipeg, I continued to keep in communication with my mother. I ventured one trip out to see her in Penticton. She stopped drinking for three days because my trip mattered to her. Her second husband, El, told me how hard it was for her to suddenly stop drinking. She had one glass eye by then due to a fall while intoxicated, but she still made efforts to take pride in herself.

I noticed the forty-plus knife gouges in their bedroom door. I knew exactly what had been going on over the years between them and El didn't want to say much about it. He had moved himself down to the basement.

Mom and I had several good conversations in the three days I was there. She revealed many things to me including her own confusion regarding her own sexuality. She had stored away many articles from magazines and newspapers in her bedroom about homosexuality. As I revealed more of my sexuality with her she also told me about being attracted to women in the past, especially one of her close female friends whom I recalled very well. I had actually suspected at one point that my mother was a bisexual woman who never had an opportunity to talk about it to anyone, until that moment with me. It must have been so confusing for her.

In our time together in her sobriety, I again felt her emotional depth and her desire to give love. I felt her genuine feisty spirit and her deep longing to be understood. She wanted to be loved and appreciated for the efforts she had made in trying to provide for us in the past years. Nothing she could say could quickly dissolve the impact of her violence. Truthfully, I knew she didn't remember everything she had done and I'm sure part of her didn't want to remember. Yet, she also wanted to be accepted and forgiven.

She told me she knew she had been a "bad mother." I listened to her with more openness and compassion. The distance between us with my years in Winnipeg had also allowed me more objectivity. She wanted to share what she had learned in her life with me. She was from a whole other generation and her opportunities had been far more limited than mine. I looked at her life and I sensed she would be going soon. It saddened me. I realized clearly she had never been equipped to be the mother that any of us had needed. In all of her fears, confusion and illness, she gave as much as she could. I returned to Winnipeg with a softened, more forgiving heart and I wondered if I would ever see her again.

A few months later Mom wrote me a letter. She reflected on her marriage and her feelings about herself. In part of it she wrote:

"I don't need to live in a closet—or feel guilty. I need fresh air, laughter, people who care. Needing to feel secure. That is the time I can go forth and help others. I feel I have the warmth in me anyway. I love to dance (same as you). I believe God gave you the ability to care, love and be loved. <u>Feel Loved</u> and you will be. Love is the key note.

"Mom"

Deep down, she did understand the importance of love. Underlying all of her behaviour was her desire to be heard and to be loved. In her reaching out, her words felt important to me.

One day I heard my mother's voice on the answering machine. I said to my partner at the time, "my mother will die in two weeks." "How do you know that?" she said.

"I just know."

I was right. Two weeks, later at age sixty-four, my mother died from a heart attack. I had anticipated her death for years with a sense of dread and suspended grief—it was always on my mind. Still, it was a terrible blow. My world was turned upside down.

Into the Fire

Though shocked by her death, I also knew I was freer to examine and let go of my relationship with my mother. I once again chose to go "into the fire."

I knew it would be deeply painful to review my life with my mother as I had already gone through two years of wrenching therapy in the past. However, I was firmly committed to seeing myself through this significant loss. I was prepared to face another level of emotional upheaval in order to more fully release her impact upon my life.

Grief Work

Every day I spent at least one hour of scheduled "grief time" alone, played music that opened my heart, pored over family pictures and journals and followed the direction of a resource book at the time called *Life After Loss* (Deitz, 1988). It greatly assisted me.

After about six months I felt more emotionally and psychically released. However, as with my brother's death, it contributed to my separating myself out of a relationship with a woman I really cared for. My world was changing. I became restless and felt I had to move on.

I became involved with a woman visiting from Whitehorse, Yukon, and another adventure was set in motion that would further contribute to my spiritual, emotional and professional growth.

More Transitions

My move to the Yukon Territory where I became employed as an Alcohol and Drug Counsellor lasted for three years. It was a time of necessary learning. Being faced on a daily basis in assisting addicted people to recover was not only facing my parents and developing a greater understanding and compassion for them, but also developing that for myself.

My time in the Yukon ended and I chose to return to Vancouver to finish my Masters Degree in Social Work.

With part-time work not supporting me well enough upon my return to Vancouver, I took a course in teaching English as a Second Language. My spirit felt buoyed as I enjoyed the creativity in this teaching area. I would soon apply for a job and within five weeks I was accepted and transferred to teach in Seoul, Korea.

After fourteen months in Seoul, I returned to Vancouver, BC, which would become my permanent home. Of course, more spiritual, personal and professional challenges would follow. In shifting my professional pursuits and entering new relationships, I would grow more consciously aware of my relationship with Spirit, and Spirit in turn would encourage me to go even deeper within.

CHAPTER 2

OPENING YOUR HEART

*"Here is my secret. It is very simple:
It is only with the heart that one can see rightly; what is essential is invisible to the eye."*
(Saint-Exupery, 1943)

Deciding to Open

I have always believed in how my heart feels since I was a very young child. All through my life, I've listened to it.

Many people don't trust their hearts. An open heart is a healthy heart. When you can discern what your heart's messages are beyond your ego's demands and your mind's confusing statements, you will know your heart is indeed trustworthy. It has both innocence and an undaunted strength.

Opening my heart is always a physical, emotional and spiritual experience. It is where I feel most connected to the loving spiritual energy that surrounds me. When

I open my heart I feel forgiving, compassionate and accepting toward myself and others. I feel more energized and positive. There is an increased sense of ease and flow. I can hear my inner guidance more clearly.

Consciously opening ourselves can feel challenging though, if our hearts have been significantly hurt in any way. We may have a tendency to want to remain closed in order to preserve the sense of safety. We have the right to the processes we need to take in deciding what feels right and when. However, feeling you want to be more open can be your own heart and spirit telling you it's time to do that with gentleness.

Giving is Receiving

I have learned from my life's experiences that "giving" is also about simultaneously "receiving." A simple act of giving a compliment or a smile to someone can uplift you. These small examples are where we easily experience the reciprocity of giving and receiving in action. This act is really part of a universal law in action.

Sometimes when I've felt closed in hurt and resentment, I've had to encourage myself to extend myself and give that smile. Any focus on anger becomes immediately diminished at that moment. My heart then opens to give more.

I was taught at a young age that I should always bring something when I visit anyone, something small if I can. It's brought me joy to be able to give something to someone without expectation. Our universe operates through "dynamic exchange." (Chopra, 1994) When there is an *intention* to create happiness for others it will ultimately create happiness for you.

There are other situations where giving positive thought can result in receiving or achieving better results.

Whenever I enter into any social or professional gathering that could be challenging for various reasons, I do it with the conscious intent of "giving" in the way of being supportive of all present and keeping myself open to listen. In advance I send light and love into the setting I'll be entering. If there is potential for discord then I imagine a positive resolution. When you focus your positive thoughts in advance for all concerned, you will move yourself into a higher energetic frequency. You will stand a far better chance at managing yourself and witnessing a more positive outcome for everyone concerned.

This practice is especially effective in gatherings where there are conflicting agendas, misunderstandings or personality issues. The positive goodwill that you have forwarded in advance combined with the energy you arrive with will be felt by others. Our egos have less chance of operating at full strength when positive regard is present.

Gratitude

Another way of experiencing this "giving/receiving" reciprocity is in giving gratitude for that which we already have. It can be another simple way to open your heart and mind.

Get your feelings involved when you think of what you're thankful for and what it would be like if you *didn't* have that particular item or person in your life. If you have a job or any possessions you value, express your appreciation. I feel grateful that I have eyes to see the beauty of nature around me and ears to hear music I love; I am grateful for the sense of a breeze or the touch of a loving friend.

Before you get your day started or before you retire at night, giving thought to what you are grateful for can set a positive tone for your day and for your rest at night.

It's important to try to remember to acknowledge and give appreciation for *yourself*. You have already demonstrated courage and lovingness in so many ways you may not be aware of. Your very presence has created important lessons for others who have met you.

I find I am constantly saying "thank you" to Spirit when I am aware I have just missed a bad accident, found a great parking spot, saw or heard something that emotionally moved me, spent time with someone I care about or just learned something new. It really can be anything that I know that has just been a gift or an opportunity that's come my way.

In the expression of gratitude, you will find that you will begin to feel uplifted for longer periods. Your entire being will hear you.

Prayer

I do use a form of prayer. It changed from my Christian childhood roots to the knowledge that I am co-creating my life with Spirit—the Intelligent Universal power that surrounds me. I do not see a separation between myself and the energy and positive life force that is expressed in all of nature. I feel we are all infinitely connected to this spiritual energy.

Silver Birch, a Spirit Guide, through the mediumship of an Englishman named Maurice Barbanell, talks about the value of prayer:

> *"Prayer is the means by which you attune yourself to higher forces. I do not mean by prayer repeating the words that others have written without a realization of what they mean, but praying with the soul and the mind, with an earnest desire to reach out to the highest the soul can attain. Then, filled with the inspiration that comes as a result of the prayer, you emerge stronger."*
> (Silver Birch, 2008)

When I find myself in a state of prayerfulness and gratitude, a spiritual energy beyond my own being comes into play. It feels transcendent. Then I surrender or let go and expect to be guided to the solution. Some requests are answered almost instantaneously and some requests will take time. I always receive the help I need.

There is a Rune, "Sowelu," meaning "Wholeness, Life Forces and The Sun's Energy," that offers a prayer I am fond of. The prayer is known as Gayatri and it says:

> *"You, who are the source of all power,*
> *Whose rays illuminate the whole world,*
> *Illuminate also my heart,*
> *So that it too can do Your work"*
> (Blum, 1987)

Sending Prayer to Another

I am always sending prayer and positive regard to anyone whom I know needs it. I feel prayer is a natural gift to be given.

The benefits of sending prayer or positive energy have already been proven. There is much scientific evidence available that tells us that when we align our minds and hearts with the loving energy of Spirit we become open channels through which the unlimited universal spiritual energy can pass and help the person we are praying for.

We all can transmit or send positive loving energy and it will sometimes dramatically aid in healing body, mind and spirit. I don't believe anyone needs to be perfectly resolved or healed to help heal anyone else. All that is required to transmit healing to another is simple loving concern. We can all act as healers at any moment in time. We can even send healing to those who have passed on to Spirit, for their consciousness can receive us there as well. Spirit connects to our spirit no matter the dimension.

Dossey (1989), with respect to the importance of Love in healing others, acknowledges that although the medical system is changing, the "most elaborate (medical) treatment algorithms ... never contain a box that says 'LOVE' or 'CARE!' And that is why the algorithms fail. And that is also the reason why computers, flow diagrams, and all decision-making charts can never duplicate the job of a healer."

Bernie Siegel (1989) also notes in his work with many people suffering from life-threatening and debilitating diseases that his own ability to show love to his clients is the most significant aspect of his work in helping people love and heal themselves.

When I walk in my neighbourhood or at the ocean wall near my home, I often offer quietly within to strangers the words "peace to you," "bless you" or "love to you" as they pass by. If I see someone who seems in need or appears distressed, I call on Spirit to help them. I also send friends and family light and love and I imagine them surrounded by white light that is protective, healing and uplifting. It is a non-invasive, positive thing to do.

To be sure, although some gestures may seem small, our thoughts are real things and may well tip the balance toward healing and resolution for that person or that situation in the very moment you send them those loving thoughts. We can all use a little extra help with something.

It's a good way of keeping yourself in a compassionate, caring consciousness to hear your own guidance. It's a way of continuing to invest in the "Good Will Bank"—by investing in the natural law of reciprocity. These positive gestures will then be sent back to you in time. Good vibes are contagious.

Many Expressions of Love and Healing

Most of us have read passages or words of inspiration that resonate to our spirit and make us feel stronger, more open and happier. Reading passages on a daily basis that inspire love, compassion and gratitude will boost your energy.

My own previous training for many years as a therapist and now in Reiki healing is also powerful in helping me stay open and use myself as a conduit in connection to the healing energies. Spirit's intelligence knows exactly where anyone needs healing.

Maintaining my heart and mind in an open state helps Spirit's healing power do its work. This is part of Spirit's nature and allows me, as a healer, to work in perfect synergy with the client's, my own and Spirit's energies. The information that comes through to me from Spirit in thought, word or image is a perfect blend of all our energies. Divinity without connects to Divinity within.

In helping others in this wonderful process I can immediately feel myself receiving healing. The experience is powerfully unmistakable. I feel joyful, centred and peaceful, and my energy is vibrantly increased for hours.

Tarot, Runes and other forms of divination that summon my spirit's wisdom have helped to keep me centred and open.

Music, Voice, Movement

Universally we can easily appreciate the value of music and rhythm that inspires us or invites us to sing, dance or make love—it's an important part of creating heart openings and uplifting our spirits. I've used gentle music throughout the writing of this book. It significantly helped keep me open and allowed Spirit's information to come through me. When I got tired or stuck, I'd go outside to be in nature. You can shift your thoughts and mood for the better by simply getting yourself up and moving.

When I was a child I would sing a special song many times over and I would ask my sister, Lindsay, to sing with me as we walked up the street, garnering stares from our neighbours with our resounding voices. Fortunately, she loved to sing too.

The song we sang was called, "You'll Never Walk Alone," and it is an old 1945 show tune from R. Rogers and O.

Hammerstein's *Carousel*. Some of you may have heard it before. It was my fourth grade teacher's favourite song and it became one of my favourite songs, even to this day. It still inspires me and opens my heart as it did then. I give it to you:

"When you walk through the storm
Hold your head up high
And don't be afraid of the dark
At the end of the storm
There's a golden sky
And the sweet silver song of the lark

"Walk on, through the wind
Walk on, through the rain
Though your dreams be tossed and blown
Walk on, walk on, with hope in your heart
And you'll never walk alone
You'll never walk alone

"Walk on, walk on, with hope in your heart
And you'll never walk alone
You'll never walk alone"

CHAPTER 3

YOUR HEART'S DESIRES

Our Beliefs

When I was a child I was an avid reader. I constantly read science fiction that often did not feel like fiction at all. I travelled well with the author's imagination and tended to believe that anything was possible. I read all the *Black Stallion* stories that usually had some sense of triumph over adversity.

When I was twelve years old, my interest also involved delving into ancient stories of Atlantis and Lemuria, with the archaeological and some very old "channelled" writings of the amazing technological feats of these ancient people. These stories fascinated me and spurred my imagination.

Perhaps in being a Sagittarius, I also naturally tended toward contemplating limitless possibilities on a regular basis. Part of me always remained idealistic and adventurous in believing I could accomplish almost anything.

Our beliefs formed in earlier childhood have powerful and direct impacts on what we are drawing into our lives. These beliefs colour what is possible for us to achieve and are reflected back to us in our thoughts, words and behaviours.

Listening to our thoughts, our words and our body's reactions to situations can bring greater conscious awareness to many of the core beliefs we've grown up with. If we listen closely to ourselves and take note of our behaviours, we can begin to discern what our core beliefs are. We can look at our beliefs in what we value.

We all have beliefs related to our self-perceptions, our worthiness to receive abundance and love and our feelings about intimate relationships. We can gradually decide if these beliefs still hold true to serve our highest good or not.

Choose to be brutally honest with yourself and expunge the beliefs that do not support you. Substitute opposite beliefs—ones that support you and increase your sense of self-esteem and wellness; beliefs that tell you that you are successful and can do anything you put your mind to. You will reap the benefits.

Over many years from examining my beliefs, listening to myself and knowing I wanted changes, I found that there are tried-and-true key points for creating those changes and manifesting what I really wanted to see in my life. These key areas include:

- Disciplining your thoughts for the positive
- Using your words as power tools

SPIRITUAL INTELLIGENCE 67

- Creating a list of what you really want
- Using the power of your imagination
- Affirming that you have received your desire
- Letting go
- Being open to receiving what you are asking for
- Setting time aside
- Maintaining silence
- Dealing with doubt

In more detail, here's how it works:

Our Thoughts

What do we think about? We have ideas about what we want. However, we often get sidetracked and think more about what we *don't want or don't have.* Focussing on what we don't want, or don't have, will reinforce the energy of that particular situation returning, thus re-creating a sense of lack.

Never mind the past mistakes and regrets. Accept your losses, forgive yourself and let it go. Accept you did the best you could in each circumstance. Otherwise, the "shoulda, coulda, woulda" will continue to harass and torment you. This thinking will contribute to fear and will erode your true power in the moment.

Many people are motivated by fear. When this happens we get out of touch with our own present moment. We get pulled into focussing on the past or the future. Focus on what you want and stay positive and *present* with that focus.

Power in Words

How often do we positively acknowledge and affirm ourselves? Do you practice telling yourself that you can accomplish anything you put your mind to? Do you congratulate yourself on your day's achievements? Or do you tell yourself, "Well, I didn't do that very well today," or, "I'm not that smart," or, "I never have time to do what I really want."

Don Miguel Ruiz, author of *The Four Agreements* (1997), emphasizes the power of the spoken word as a "gift from God"—an essential tool in humanity's code of conduct. He writes that, with the right use of words, we can either enslave people or set them free.

It's true, our words have the power to uplift, to heal, to encourage. Power to be truthful. Power to extend caring and compassion. Power to injure or to violate. Power to build our energy and power to diminish it.

We can increase our energy and self-esteem in a moment by what we think and what we say. Our thoughts and words are extremely potent and are creating our realities on a continuous basis. Start by changing your internal dialogue about yourself and you will feel immediate change.

Give yourself direct positive messages. I have notes with short affirmations at work and at home to keep me focussed on the positives in life and to also remind me to "Allow," "Listen Within" and "Go with the Flow."

I will telephone myself messages if I need to remind myself of something important and I'll take that opportunity to tell myself "how wonderful I am, how much I love and accept myself; that I am successful, loving and strong and that everything is unfolding as it should." Some wouldn't consider this verbal self-acknowledgment as anything of importance, but when you hear *your own voice* supporting and encouraging you, as your own best friend, you'll feel better than you did a few minutes earlier. It works!

An example of an overall power statement that uplifts me is: *"I am strong, healthy, youthful, wealthy, successful and happy."* I'll alter it according to what I feel I need in that moment.

My understanding with what I have experienced and learned over the years is that each of us has been given the *right* to decree, the spiritual authority to request what we want. It has always been part of our birthright as spiritual beings. I believe that when we recognize this authority and request what we want from our spiritual selves, we are using our energy and our power in the clearest way to bring our wishes to fruition.

Create a List of What You Want

There is metaphysical understanding that in order for us to be requesting something or a situation to manifest, then that situation already exists in our inner spirit to be materialized in the outer world. When we really want something that is in harmony with our spiritual nature and will not harm us or anyone else, then it is usually a sign that our own spirit is nudging us to pay attention.

Look inside your heart and ask what it is you truly want. Feel what conditions in your life will make you feel joyful or bring you the success you deserve. Focus on the positive in what you want, not what you don't want.

For example, focussing *solely* on reducing your financial debt will likely not reduce your debt as quickly as you'd like, or not at all. It could increase it. Do what is responsible and necessary and create a sound payment plan. Then refocus more of your attention in connecting with others who can help stimulate new ideas or can assist you in furthering your skills toward increasing your abundance. Consciously open yourself up to more possibilities.

Never mind if an idea initially seems to you to be impossible. Don't discard it or dismiss it. Write your identified wishes down in order of importance.
- Make your list as detailed as you want.
- Change it as you shift the vision of your desire.

Imagination

Our imaginations are powerful. Here's what has worked for me and others:
- Envision yourself receiving what you really want.
- Really see it happening NOW.
- Picture the successful outcome you want in as much detail as you can.
- Feel it happening. When you do this, you get your energy moving in the right direction. Your mind, feelings and imagination interconnect to boost your magnetism.

Some people use their imagination to create a vision board with pictures, drawings or anything visual that keeps them focussed on their heart's wishes. It is a good power tool.

Reflecting on what you already know you have successfully brought into your life—material wealth, job competitions you won or new ventures you successfully created—can boost your self-esteem in the moment and carry you forward. You did it, you can feel good about your accomplishment and you can do it again by using the same formula.

Affirming Your Desires

An affirmation is being firm in your statement, in your resolve. Use your words specifically to affirm the desires you really want to see come alive for you.
- Use words that have meaning for you and that you have a *feeling* for.
- Repeat your affirmation often with feeling and conviction. The more you repeat a statement to yourself and say it with feeling and conviction the more you will believe it, until one day you will say it, and it will be so.
- Affirm your wishes by telling yourself that you have *already* received the object, or that the situation has already worked out to your utmost satisfaction. Say it to yourself as if you've just received it *in this very moment*. Make it feel real to yourself and you will pull in that which you need to move you toward your dream, until it finally happens. For example:

"I'm happy that _____ has now happened," or, "It feels great that I've now completed my _____," or, "I'm happy there is resolution and peace between me and _____"

Gawain (2002), Wilde (1987) and Hicks (2004) are only a few of many authors that provide further examples for using specific mental imagery and affirmations to produce the kind of results you want in manifesting your heart's desires.

Letting Go

Once you've identified your wishes, pictured them, felt them and affirmed that they already happened, release them to Spirit. Let them go and move your mind on to something else.

Timing is everything. We will receive our heart's desires in the right time and in the right way. When we are truly ready and when the energies surrounding the circumstances are in alignment it will happen. There is never a need to push or try to *make* anything happen. If you find yourself doing this, stop.

Taming our egos and practicing patience is necessary in the long run. Spiritual Intelligence knows how, when and where your wishes will come to you. It knows without your checking to see how things are going. Letting go is ultimately about *choosing* to trust. It takes practice.

Be Ready to Receive

Ensure you are open to receiving what you are asking for. Know that you are worthy to receive the goodness you want to see in your life. Being ready and willing to accept the condition, object, person or situation you ask for is absolutely vital.

If you feel hesitant to receive what you want, perhaps you should take a deeper look into the situation. You may not be emotionally ready to receive or you might not quite have all the information you need to feel comfortable should it arrive. Explore it until it is more clear to you.

Spiritual Intelligence operates most quickly with a decisive mind.

You can affirm to yourself your ability to receive by saying, " I now welcome _____ into my life" or "I am happy to receive _____ into my life."

Setting Time Aside

It's recommended that you set time aside to read your list for about fifteen minutes or more, three times a day:
- In the morning as you set your energy level
- Sometime in mid-day
- Before you retire to sleep

If you can spend the time during these periods of the day to remind yourself of what you want to bring into your life, you will help yourself keep focussed and open. Do what works for you. I have found some days are extremely busy and that having a semblance of a schedule of brief retreat, to just be with myself to regroup and refocus, has helped me.

Maintaining Silence

Maintaining silence is another important part of manifestation. Sharing too much about what you're seeking can decrease your magnetic energy. Containing your energy and maintaining a degree of privacy will build the magnetism and assist you in more effectively pulling in your new circumstances.

Here's an example of a manifestation:

Before I moved to Whitehorse I visited there for about a week. During that time I had the opportunity to meet several Counsellors at the Drug and Alcohol Centre. I had a very positive feeling for the people and wanted to work there, but I was also told that I could not become employed anywhere in the Yukon unless I lived there.

When I returned to Winnipeg I put it in the back of my mind but the good feeling about that job persisted. So I wrote down this job on my "wish list." I also included the amount of money I wanted to receive, which was substantially more than what I was receiving at my present location.

A couple of weeks later my friend in the Yukon sent me a notice for a nationally advertised job for a Social Work position in Whitehorse. It was a job I normally would never have heard about and it was not a position I'd considered returning to. However, I felt spiritually guided to apply for this position as aspects of it were appealing. I was flown up to Whitehorse, interviewed and soon became the successful candidate. I signed a three-year contract to stay and several months later I was transferred there. Well, that was the good news.

The bad news was that three months after arriving, I was on the brink of emotional exhaustion. I understood clearly then why the other Social Worker had resigned from this post. I didn't know what on earth I was going to do, as I'd signed that three-year contract and to break it would really cost me financially. I felt stuck. Suddenly at work one day, one of my colleagues approached me with a newspaper ad I had not seen. It was for a counselling position at the Drug and Alcohol Centre. She said, "I immediately thought of you when I saw this ad because I know you love to do group work!" I was surprised and thrilled.

I applied and became an Addictions Counsellor at the very place I had really wanted all along, and began to receive the wage I had put in my wish list!

Dealing with Doubt

Do not cave into doubt if it arises. This is usually the voice of the fearful ego or your frightened inner child. Be comforting and gentle with yourself and let yourself know that "it's ok to feel doubt, its natural," and, "*I can do it.*"

Doubt can also be the voice of someone in the past who may have told you, "you'll never do it," or, "you don't have the ability to do that." This is not the voice of your spirit; it is not your true authentic self.

You can also reframe it all by saying to yourself, "Who am I to think I cannot do it, or cannot receive that!? I deserve all the goodness the world has to offer!" Remember you are connected to the eternal energy, which knows you and will give you what you want. Stay the course.

When in doubt:
- REFOCUS on your wishes.
- BREATHE deeply and move yourself back into the present moment.
- AFFIRM yourself with conviction, and tell yourself, "I can do it," and, "I will *not* accept any other thoughts that pull me away from my centre." Call on Spirit to assist you to be strong and open your heart and mind to receive this extra energy.
- IGNORE the present state of affairs you want to change. Do not focus on the way something currently is. Push your mind past it and focus on what you want the situation to look like.

- REMIND yourself that *you are in charge of your own life*. You are the power because you are directly connected to the great power source that surrounds you. You are fully capable of accomplishing whatever you put your focussed mind to.

You can build trust in yourself and in your ability to consciously co-create your life as you want to see it unfold. This is really true. Go at this practice with wilful intention. Be committed in your desire to succeed, because you will. Don't give up!

CHAPTER 4

ALLOWING AND TRUSTING

I am someone who, at an early age, had to appreciate that I must be completely responsible in looking out for and trusting myself, because my parents were in emotional distress and unable to fully provide for me. This was a good thing in a way because it made me look to my inner guidance, my intuition, to lead me. Though I learned to trust myself a lot, I was still going to have to learn to let go and trust Spirit to do more for me, rather than my doing it all, and doing it for everyone else too. I still had to learn to let go even when I was afraid.

When we let go and allow things to unfold naturally, we allow the Universe's natural flow to enter our lives more easily. We feel less stressed and pressured. Whatever we need in the moment will materialize in time, opportunities, money and people with the perfect suggestions to carry us forward.

This is the area of intuition, divinity and natural miracles. It is the area of amazing coincidence or synchronicity. It is the "what are the odds that could ever happen?!" type of experiences.

Synchronicity

This is a word with many connotations. It means "coincidence," "serendipity" or a form of intuition that we have acted upon. I believe that synchronicity really is an ongoing natural human experience.

I've always found coincidences and synchronistic moments fascinating. As I look back on my life, I can see the amazing twists and turns of events that were positive, painful and sometimes scary. These interconnected moments have moved me from one important life event to another. It's often seemed like it's all "meant to be."

I've had chance meetings with people who lead me to a resource in exactly the right time, or have told me exactly what I needed to hear in that very moment. Books that appear, words I hear, something that suddenly catches my attention for a moment or the thoughts of someone that pop into my head and suddenly I see or hear from that person.

I've taken the time to choose to notice the synchronistic patterns that emerge because there are themes that speak to me about where I want to go, what's good for me, what feels right and what doesn't feel right.

The more I notice "sheer coincidence" and synchronicities, the more I see a noticeable exchange of communication I am having with my own guiding spirit and Universal energy. This relationship has been apparent all my life. It's as if the Universe, or Spirit, has been telling me:

"I am right here and I am part of you. I am listening to your thoughts and your heart's wishes and I'm already working with you in every moment, creating all of it here and now. I'm trying to bring to you what you really want—what's best for you. Be aware of me and see the signs I am posting for you to show you where to go next. You are loved."

<u>Attending Strengthens</u>

What we pay attention to usually gains in strength in our lives. I believe that consciously noticing synchronistic patterns will provide more synchronicity to emerge around us, offering greater opportunities to draw in the energies and co-create what we really want in easier ways. This is Universal Spiritual energy speaking to us.

We can begin to make our lives easier by going with the flow and not worrying about the ways and means our heart's wishes will come to us. Instead, stay open and present, go inside and listen for direction.

Choose to observe what's coming toward you. It will help guide you. Never pressure yourself, but just gently notice how you are being shown pathways to follow. Each step is illuminated for you as you go. You only need to take the first step toward what you want and Spirit will show you the second step to take. I have seen this in my life many times. It never fails.

Walking by the ocean near my home or going to other places where people stroll is fun for synchronistic experiences. As people pass by in their conversations with each other, it is not unusual to receive an answer to a question, or have an aspect about a situation reflected back to me that gives me extra insight.

Our Guiding Inner Voice

Our inner voice has many names and definitions, from "God" to our "intuition," our "Higher Self," "Guides" or "Angels." It's just up to each one of us to figure that part out.

I've relied on my intuition ever since I was a young child because I felt I was being spiritual guided. Generally speaking, if we acknowledge the use of "intuition," it means "instinctive" or a sense of "knowing" that seems beyond the rational mind.

My inner guiding voice has come to me in several ways—as a literal, physical "gut sense" or an overall experience of being in tune and where things "feel right." My guidance has also come to me in dreams. The richness of that inner world has shown itself in words, pictures, symbols and images.

In order for me to access my inner guidance it is helpful for me to be still enough to listen. On the other hand I don't believe it is a locked-in requirement that the only way you can hear your guidance is by being totally peaceful, calm and still. Let's face it. Sometimes things happen that plain scare us or just create a lot of anxiety in the moment. It can be a tall order to "hurry up and get calm" so we can hear our guidance. Guidance can still come to us in more intense times of need. We just need to be open.

Breathing

What has helped me in moments of anxiety is to just breathe deeply in the moment. Deep breathing immediately changes the activity of the brain. It slows our brain down to an alpha state where immediate systemic calm can begin.

SPIRITUAL INTELLIGENCE

As soon as we do deep breathing we are able to relax, open more and hear our inner wisdom.

<u>Intention to Listen</u>

It is also important to have the *intention* to listen and be open to *accept* what our inner voice or intuition is telling us. If something comes to me and it seems laden with fear, rather than a gentler sense of "yes, this feels right," then I know it's usually my fearful mind instructing me, not my intuition.

My mind, being more influenced by my ego's relationship with fear, can distract me with its complexities in wanting to analyse everything ad nauseam. The ego's questions are endless as it seeks to know everything in advance as a means to ensure security and often to control the outcome of situations. Try not to let it get in your way.

Meditation

Rather than exercise, some people find they can acquire inner stillness and receive guidance through meditation. I admit I was never in tune with this method. It has been an area of challenge for me as I am a physical person who's been used to coming to calm and peacefulness through intense exercise.

However, over time I accepted other forms of meditation to reach stillness and receptivity, which proved very helpful. Guided meditation tapes are very useful and easy— as are creative writing, drawing or any other concentrated, focussed work that shifts your focus to create the openness you need.

Dreams

I have always had an extraordinary, rich dream life. In fact it has been prolific, instructional and prophetic at times. I believe this is an area where I have a natural gift—one that I've cultivated for many years. I've paid close attention to my dream life and it has been a place of communication from countless people, animals and guides, where I've been given insights into my own and others' states of distress or wellness.

In dreams I have found myself in classrooms in what appear to be university-type settings, where I am being taught spiritual lessons, shown geographical and technical maps or given guidance from what appear to be beings of light.

My unconscious has also come through in my dream life to assist me in resolving issues within myself or with other people by bringing these issues to my attention with specific symbols, language and humour that I am open to.

I have spent time with people that I am aware I've had previous relationships with. I recall a table being set for me in an old wooden cabin. There were three others present and when I came in, they greeted me with love and warmth and showed me where my place was set at the table. I conversed with this familiar family and I was perfectly aware of my surroundings inside and outside the cabin. I awoke and wondered if I had appeared as a ghost to them, or if in fact I had travelled back in time. I felt it was the latter. The spirit realm does not deal with linear time as we have on this plane. I do believe we can travel back and forth in time, in spirit.

I have also consistently conversed with my deceased brother, mother, father and other souls who have passed on from this earth plane. It seems when we are in this dream state it is easier for our loved ones to communicate with us if we are open. This is a normal occurrence for many people and one that I accept with gratitude.

As only one example, when my deceased brother, Rob, appeared in one of my dreams, the quality of the dream was spectacular. The colour of the trees, the sky, the flowers and even the walkway was distinct and immensely vibrant.

I asked him how he was doing "over there." We hugged and then walked arm in arm down a beautiful pathway. He told me he was happy and that he was healing. He said he was learning many things. I asked him if he was aware of my life and my various relationships. He told me all my relationships were for my personal growth and that they were "sacred." It was a short dream and he suddenly told me he had to go. I woke up feeling happy with immense gratitude and love for him and the gift of this experience. I felt I had really spent time with him in my dream state.

I have also dreamed of many of my own past lives and met people I've been previously involved with who have been culturally different than where I am now.

When you acknowledge your dream life as a valuable source of information and inspiration, you'll increase your ability to tap into this wealthy realm of important information about yourself, and you can receive more information that can help guide your life.

Over time you may even notice that you'll have lucid dreams, where you're aware of your dream while you are dreaming it. You can also become proficient at orchestrating your dream as you want it to be while you're dreaming. To me, these experiences have been examples from my dream life that give me reminders as to my ability to co-create with the Universal energy in my waking state.

Dreams have been invaluable in showing me themes, prophetic information and warnings. The warnings in dreams have come in various forms, from small warnings to warnings about major, life-altering events, sometimes for me and sometimes for others. Here is an example:

While I lived in the Yukon working as a child protection Social Worker, I had the opportunity to work with two teenage sisters, ages fifteen and seventeen. One still lived with her mother while the other lived in a foster home. They had been telling me that they wanted to go to visit their father in Kelowna, BC. These two sisters were good friends as they had survived a great deal of emotional hardship with their family's breakup.

I had a dream in which these sisters were travelling to their destination. I saw them in a car accident as passengers with their foster mother. Both girls were killed. I woke up startled and very concerned as the dream felt real to me. I wondered if I should say anything to the supervisor or the girls. I had learned, though, to take my dreams and their symbols seriously as being a legitimate form of communication from my inner guidance.

I went to the supervisor that day and told her exactly my dream and that I recommended the girls not travel to the Okanagan, at least not by car. I suggested they wait for a change in circumstances or that they fly down if they insisted on going. The supervisor was open and in the end the decision was mine to speak about this dream or not.

I had a good relationship with this family and I decided that I would reveal my dream and my grave concern for their personal safety should they travel by car. They listened but their minds were made up. The trip had been planned for a long time.

They left on their destination. Our office heard a day later that they had been in a terrible car accident with a truck and one sister had died and the other was critically injured. I felt sick inside but I also knew I had done what I could do to stop them from taking that route.

Dream Journals

It's been very worthwhile to write my dreams in journals. Even if you think you don't dream or cannot remember your dreams, you can shift that by attending to any details you wake up with. A good thing to do is to pay attention to what you dreamed and how you *felt* when you awakened. Those feelings will give you a clue as to what you dreamed and contribute to more development on your part in recalling your dreams.

Guiding Entities

Through many years of being involved in different spiritual study groups, listening to channelled messages from wonderful and reputable healers in my life, I have chosen to believe that I may also have Spiritual Guides. I believe that they know me well and are aware when I need assistance. All I do is ask for help.

Some people call these entities "Angels" or even loved ones that have passed on and choose to stay connected to us. Some people may have other known cultural, religious or spiritual figures that they believe are with them for guidance. Whatever we believe in has power in our lives.

Whether the guidance has been from within me as my intuition or from another spiritual plane from guiding entities, I find that communication within me is usually gentle and comes in a way that makes sense to me.

Here's a small example of a tenuous time for me and the way I worked in listening to and following my guidance:

I had left full-time employment and was on Employment Benefits while I was doing my Masters degree in Social Work. My mother suddenly passed away. Even though I had a premonition of her death I was deeply shocked and grief stricken. I felt vulnerable and my self-confidence was shaken.

Prior to her death, I had the opportunity to be hired for several jobs that, unfortunately, I considered obvious burnout positions, so I declined them. I had made a promise to myself that I would choose further employment that would be healthier for me and less emotionally exhausting.

One day I woke up and realized I had only one Employment Benefit cheque left. I would not be able to pay my rent or have sufficient food for myself or my two cats. I felt very anxious as my worst nightmare was clearly swiftly approaching. I sat for a while to calm myself and wondered, "was I mistaken to turn down those other jobs?" I was also certain with all my research that there were no other jobs available in the city.

I really didn't know what to do, so I did what I needed to do in the moment. I went for a run to burn off my anxiety at the indoor track nearby. I knew that in running I'd put myself in a more relaxed state.

When I'd finished my run, it came to mind that I should drop by and say "hello" to Susan who had hired me one time as a Crisis Counsellor for the Canadian Mental Health Association. Susan was always very busy but just happened to have time to sit for a chat. After barely a minute she bluntly stated, "I've been thinking about you and wondering why you haven't applied for that job on the board? I know the pay isn't great but we'd love to have you! I think you'd enjoy it."

I was surprised as I had no idea the job existed and it was not posted anywhere. I immediately knew it was the right thing to do so I went ahead and applied on the spot.

I received the job a few days later, and true, the pay was considerably lower than I'd been seeking but the expectations were more than reasonable for me given my state of vulnerability. My prayers had truly been answered. This job turned out to be the perfect transitional position for me at a difficult time of my life. I had also honoured my word to choose a healthy job for me.

What Helped in that Moment?

In retrospect, without even giving it much thought, I had done some things that worked to assist me in pulling that position in:

1. **Returning to the present moment.** The first thing I did was to sit with myself and get back to the

present moment. I checked my feelings to see what I needed to do for myself in the moment.
2. **Breathing and reducing anxiety.** I chose to do what was familiar and healthy to cope with anxiety and stress to get myself relaxed, open and clear. I decided to go for a run at an indoor track. Releasing my anxiety in intense breathing exercise helped to further calm and centre me.
3. **Listening.** Because I let go of my anxiety I was more relaxed and open. I could hear my inner guidance more easily than remaining in a tense, closed state.
4. **Choosing to follow.** I chose to follow what had come into my mind. I checked that it felt right to follow the "nudging" to visit my friend. I had no idea she had also been thinking of me.
5. **Receiving with gratitude.** Yes, I did say "thank you!" to Spirit. There were more opportunities for higher income positions that came afterward. I gradually was able to rebuild my self-confidence from that point on.

The period of time from high anxiety to a connection with information about employment for me was a four-hour process. Situations manifest in the time they are meant to and we are open to them.

Practice Empowers

The more often we practice the process I describe above of asking for help, tuning in to the present moment and staying open for any guidance, the more we will build strength and confidence for swifter manifestations. We can learn to trust ourselves to deal with any situation that comes our way. We can meet challenges in a calmer manner and end up with the results we are looking for or, sometimes, something even better.

As we consistently tap into our spirit and inner guidance our energy becomes increasingly more positive, our consciousness shifts and we stay functioning longer at a higher vibration.

Inner Guidance and Divine Intervention

One time when I was just learning how to drive, I was about to turn left onto a road way. A loud, clear voice startled me that came from my right side. It emphatically stated, *"Don't turn there!"* I immediately slowed right down as a car came careening around the corner narrowly missing me for what would have been a very serious collision. I believe this incident was an example of Angelic or "divine intervention."

Sometimes a significant, or even an injurious, event will lead us to a path we were meant to be on. Here's what I mean:

When I was an undergrad in my first year at the University of Victoria, we had one of our nights for students to let loose from the week's classes at a university dance.

My boyfriend at the time drove a small Austin Mini and no one bothered wearing seat belts. Earlier in the day before going out to a university dance, a voice within me very specifically stated, "Don't drink more than two ounces of alcohol!" I felt urgency to this message, so I paid attention and refused all drinks my partying partners were ordering for me. I felt decisive.

When the dance ended we decided to head to a local restaurant in downtown Victoria. My boyfriend decided to drive while I took the passenger seat. As we approached the entrance to Ring Road that encircled the university campus, a large Pontiac with six intoxicated students approached. It veered out of control and crossed over into our lane.

I could see the headlights coming from the Pontiac well in advance. Time slowed right down to a heartbeat. I suddenly felt an ethereal cloak drape over me and a loving presence surround me. I knew we were going to crash but I felt very calm as I waited in those few seconds.

I felt myself lift off the seat and crash head first into the windshield. As my head smashed right through the glass up to my neck, I was momentarily suspended in motion. I then came back through the windshield landing with a jolt onto my seat. I was stunned, yet calm, and sat quietly as the commotion began to unfurl. I wasn't fully aware of my injuries.

Eventually we were transferred to Victoria's Royal Jubilee Hospital. As I was being placed on a stretcher, the medical attendants realized my neck was badly cut. I learned later from the attending surgeon that I was within 1/16th of an inch of dying with a severed jugular.

I went over this event many times in my mind over the next months. The message to me was that if I had not been entirely sober I could have hit the windshield in a different position and the crash would surely have killed me or at least severely disabled me.

Career Changed

I had intended on being a Physical Education and Guidance Teacher. As it turned out, because of the injury to my neck, I was advised to not continue with my Physical Education courses. I was very disappointed that my dream career would not be fulfilled. I chose to go forward in the Guidance Counselling path.

Through a series of other synchronistic "meant to be" encounters with people who would guide me on my career path, I was led into the therapeutic, healing area of Social Work. I later realized that I was truly meant to follow this road in life.

The spiritual guidance and my decision to choose to attend to the message resulted in my life being given back to me in a new way.

Relationship with Animals

I have always felt a deep spiritual kinship with the animal kingdom. Animals not only provide comfort and protection to us but they will also provide us with direct information as to how we are currently emotionally functioning.

When I have been upset in any way my two cats have come to me in comfort. They have also been my barometers in mirroring my anger and frustrations.

Many years ago I was involved in a relationship that was unhealthy for me and created much frustration and anger within my home. I was disturbed to see the two feline brothers begin to savagely fight with each other. I knew from years living with them that they were really best friends. I eventually left that relationship, which immediately put my animals at ease.

As I have come to know animals I can feel and see how they attempt to communicate with us and how sensitive they are. Unconditional love is so easily seen in our spiritual friends. They come to us to spiritually learn and grow as much as we learn and grow with them. Relationships are never one-sided. We are all interconnected on this energetic plane. It is only our misunderstanding of their spiritual form that can stand in our way of fully respecting and seeing how and what animals can teach us. Here is a quote I want to share with you:

> *"For the animal shall not be measured by man. In a world older and more complete than our own they move finished and complete, gifted with extensions of the senses we have lost or never attained, living by voices we shall never hear. They are not brethren, they are not underlings; they are older nations, caught with ourselves in the net of life and time."*
> (Beston, 1928)

Psychics

I believe we all have spiritual gifts within us. Some of us have developed these gifts and we can learn to more finely tune into our guiding systems. The ability to more deeply intuit, feel, perceive and discern can assist in the development of clairaudience, clairvoyance, prophecy and psychometry.

I have met some wonderfully sincere and talented healers, mediums and psychics in my lifetime that have encouraged, healed and guided me. They have also assisted me with the development of my own spiritual gifts. However, I've also met a few unbalanced souls that have tested my own inner guidance whereby I've refuted what they've had to say.

I have always checked within after hearing anyone's "channelled' information to see if it feels right for me. If not, then it's put aside as with anyone's advice that feels off base.

One time I met a psychic who told me that "partying is a spiritual experience." With amusement I thought I'd never heard such wonderful truth fall from someone's lips!

Then she told me to forget about finishing my Master of Social Work degree. She said it would be a "complete waste of time and money." Needless to say, I ignored her and proceeded onward to my degree's completion. Later, in true "spiritual fashion," I celebrated!

At this moment in my life I prefer to not know how things are to turn out based on someone else's interpretation of my life. I want to be maximally in tune with myself. Otherwise, I can also get in my own way by thinking of outcomes set by another and not listen to my own sense of direction.

However, if I feel stuck or energetically blocked and unable to find clarity for myself, then I will consider the healer best suited to my needs.

Astrology

Astrology essentially involves astronomy. It deals with our individual human circumstances and the correlating events on earth in relationship to the celestial bodies that surround us. It can take an Astrologer several years to learn this wonderful study. Examining your astrology chart can give you excellent insights into why you decided to be born at this time, what your lessons are in this life and where you're headed spiritually on your journey.

When I lived in Winnipeg, Manitoba, I believe I was spiritually guided to learn about my astrological birth chart and its implications in terms of how I use my energy.

I met an intuitive woman named Marjorie, who listened to my spiritual journey and offered to give me an astrology reading. I didn't believe in this study until the initial three-hour reading was finished. I was amazed that this woman knew more about me by studying my chart than I had revealed to most people.

The sun sign, moon sign and other celestial bodies in the ten areas called "houses" were read and their interrelationships were explained to me. The shock that took place at the time of my birth and the impact of my parents on me was clearly seen in this chart, as were other specific events. As I learned astrology for myself, I understood how I used my energy in my daily communications and was able to see areas that I wanted to change. It was another way of viewing myself and others that was compassionate, enlightening and inspirational.

There are many ways to access our inner guidance that can promote our conscious awareness, self-trust and peace of mind. The Spiritual energy surrounding us can therefore run through us and manifest what we desire when we are in a clearer state of openness and non-resistance.

CHAPTER 5

YOUR CONSCIOUSNESS AS CONDUIT

Have you noticed that when you've come to emotional clearings in resolving personal issues, your life flows better?

I believe it is true that the spirit within us and that surrounds us is an infinite and intelligent energy. It seems to work best to bring us what we desire when it can work through a positive, consciously clear state of mind.

Thoughts are real things. Therefore what we put into the Universe as a thought, negative or positive, will be on its way to manifestation. We know this as the Law of Attraction. However, we can cancel out that positive thought when we are ambivalent, conflicted, critical, blaming and the like. That's when we're likely to manifest a mixed bag of experiences, not entirely to our satisfaction.

Many of us aspire to acquire a better career path, or be in a more satisfying love relationship or receive more financial abundance. Some of us have done all the visualizations, affirmations and journaling, but what we really want is still not here. We say, "This manifestation stuff doesn't work." That may be the experience for some but perhaps there is something else to consider.

There may be deeper root causes that just affirming from a mind level won't quite get to what is blocking you.

If we do want something to change more permanently that will contribute to our well being, we sometimes have to dig deeper to see what attachments or feelings might still be undermining us in our ability to receive. This was my experience.

From doing this work I know that these deeper inner journeys require courage to uncover what has hurt us or what we've judged as unacceptable about ourselves. Sometimes we'd prefer to keep specific areas hidden. But when we adopt the attitude of kindness and compassion as we explore our inner terrain, we'll see there are parts of ourselves longing to be recognized and accepted with caring attention.

The following areas are ones I've explored within myself in depth and that I continue to be mindful of.

Attachments

When I started to become interested in Buddhist teachings I became more aware of the concept of attachments and how being overly attached to things, beliefs and behaviours could sometimes bring a measure of discord into our lives.

For example it seems true that if we find ourselves holding on tightly to an insistence on wanting things "my way," it is about maintaining control sometimes at great cost. There is no real inner freedom in this position—a position based on fear. When we hold fearfully to a position in this way we may try to force a specific outcome, often through manipulative means that could well be detrimental to ourselves or another. Additionally from this place of attachment and control can also rise judgment, blame, anger, fear and self-centeredness. If it is continued, we can become emotionally separated from ourselves and others. Spiritually, it cuts us off from the awareness of the truth that we are all ultimately energetically connected.

I've examined my degree of attachment to all my possessions, my employment positions, my relationships, where I live and some of my more staunch beliefs. I've asked myself what was the degree of meaning I held to any of these attachments. If they were suddenly taken away, or I found some of my beliefs were untrue, where would that leave me and how would I view myself?

I still find this area challenging but overall being aware of becoming overly attached to anything, anyone, or any specific outcome is a signal to me that I need to re-evaluate where I am with whatever the situation is. Maybe I'm becoming rigid and therefore fearful of losing something in the end. Fear of some kind of loss is usually what I've found underneath. Whatever the fear is I do feel that examining our degree of attachments and being open to altering our perceptions and behaviour are invaluable. These acts can help us to see where we may be using an attachment that may have become entrenched into an addictive, psychological and behavioural habit. It may have become an attachment that blocks us from fully experiencing a necessary truth about ourselves or experiencing feelings we find uncomfortable.

Being Truthful About Feelings

Being honest about how we feel can be very difficult at times. But I believe it's important to recognize and support our feelings no matter what they are, whether we view them as positive and loving or whether we feel they are "negative" as in hurt, anger, fear, guilt, shame or grief. I believe that there are no negative feelings, only our judgements about them. There are feelings most of us would rather not have as they're uncomfortable and sometimes frightening.

Denying feelings, numbing them out through alcohol or other drugs or dismissing them as unimportant will stand in our way of experiencing our full strength. Being open to recognizing all feelings is about accepting an essential part of ourselves. Working with those feelings toward resolution can demand your courage and commitment.

It's not everyone's choice, but by exploring what's happened in your life with a counsellor and accessing good resource books, or participating in support groups you can help clear confusion and bring yourself clarity about experiences and feelings that need your attention.

I learned a long time ago that it actually took more energy for me to repress or stuff down my feelings than in the end to allow them their voice. That's a lot of energy in keeping something away from ourselves that wants to come out; energy we could be using elsewhere.

Abandonment

I'm highlighting this issue on its own because it is so pervasive and often not fully recognized as a core fear that is disruptive to so many people. We all fear abandonment to some degree. Abandonment is a primal fear and a universal experience.

Susan Anderson (2000), in her work, acknowledges that abandonment is still an unrecognized area of profound and legitimate grief. She describes abandonment survivors as being those who have braved through the depth of their losses and still have faith in Love's ability to enter their lives.

Learning not to abandon ourselves can be challenging if we are used to distracting ourselves with excess activities, work or anything else that allows us to avoid dealing with our losses. In doing this vital work we will significantly reduce the risk of drawing in others who abandon themselves and may also abandon us in our relationships.

In addressing this area in my own life, I found the core issue of abandonment was still present after many years. I had done much work in this area before, but there are often layers we have to go through within our lives' experiences to get all of it resolved. My own abandonment was a result of lingering, deep grief due to the profound losses in my life. With the experience of being a therapist for years, I knew what I had to do and I knew it would be hard.

I pulled out some of my reference books for this work. It took me about six months of daily focus to emotionally dig down deeper and give further release to the core areas of sadness and great grief. Many tears came with this exploration. With compassion and self-acceptance of what I had gone through in my life, my strengthening and transformation occurred.

This personal work, as difficult as it can be, will increase your emotional strength and your self-esteem, and as a result will allow more of your creative energy to return. You will gradually feel the difference and you will energetically begin to feel lighter. You'll find yourself moving forward in your life with increased confidence.

Acceptance and Forgiveness

We will only hurt ourselves and keep ourselves in a hostage state by holding onto our grudges. There is no relief. I know this from my own personal experience and lost nights of sleeps. In one moment we can feel righteous anger that energizes us, but over time, storing that toxic energy in our minds and bodies will rob us of our life force and peace of mind. Giving up resentments and allowing ourselves to move toward acceptance and forgiveness is healthier in the end.

I found that you cannot give lip service to forgiveness though. It's a process. Sometimes the process of forgiveness involves "sitting in the fire" of your pain and just staying with it until you release it. Cry it out in as much depth of heartache as it takes. This is hard work to release that pain and not expect that the person who has brought injury to you will ever acknowledge it or even be aware of it. There are times you have to just accept the situation as it is and continue to move forward in your life.

When you succeed in this work though, then you will make room for more love that *wants* to come to you, and *will* come to you. You will begin to feel a change taking place, a sense of clarity, renewed energy and lightness. This is what transformation brings.

Sometimes forgiveness can arrive in a moment of grace.

I am reminded of an experience about my father, which I will share with you.

As a teenager, I remember travelling out of my home town with my high school girls' basketball team. Our bus stopped en route and we all crowded into a little terminal restaurant, feeling excited as we looked forward to the game.

Suddenly, an inebriated, dishevelled man entered, swearing and demanding service. We all stared at him in annoyance. He'd arrived from the other bus. One of my teammates, Linda, looked over at me with wide eyes and whispered, "Barb, isn't that your father?" Linda was a neighbour and knew my father.

Emotions overwhelmed me. I recognized Dad immediately when he came in. I put my head down in humiliation. During my childhood, I'd seen him too often in this condition, and now he was doing it here, right in front of everyone. I couldn't face it.

I shook my head and quietly said, "No, it's not him."

It was a moment I could never forget. It wasn't in my nature to be dishonest and I felt I was betraying myself and my father. He was quickly escorted out of the terminal.

As the years passed since that time, I'd done a lot of healing from my own pain around missing my father and all the terrible drunken scenes. I had not ever fully forgiven him for abandoning my siblings and my mother. A part of me felt he didn't care about me.

There was something from his past before he was my father. When he was in WW II as an RCAF bombardier, his men drowned around him when his Liberator Bomber blew up off Boundary Bay, BC. He had been on a training run and a bomb had malfunctioned and exploded. He was the only survivor. He had to swim to save his own life.

It became so clear to me one day, sitting with him years later, that he had never fully recovered from his war trauma. I could not fully hear his pain until that very day when he recounted, with tears, his memory of this terrible event.

I knew he was a brilliant man who had "gone wrong," but instead of just seeing a man who drank too much, my heart heard him and my compassion came forward. In a moment I forgave him.

It was a moment I needed to have because in meeting with him that day, I saw that he was just a man who had struggled with many extraordinary and difficult life experiences, and in his own way, he was also asking for my compassion and my forgiveness.

All my anger dissolved as my heart opened and I understood him. It became a transformative, healing moment. The peace of mind and the freedom of heart that came with this experience will stay with me forever.

There are other times that we ourselves feel we need to ask for forgiveness. When we do this it can be an act of courage—an act of extending your heart to another. It is a way of taking responsibility for your actions. Your ability to extend yourself may be more important than how the other person responds. It can become a moment where you plant the seeds of acceptance and healing for you both.

Triggers

Strained moments between people come and go. Depending on how deep the involvement and attachment is to the person whom you perceived to have just slighted you, you might suddenly feel reactive—triggered off in hurt and anger. Or a perfect stranger might become "the last straw." Triggers can give you a good clue where you might still be vulnerable, where there is internal stress and where you may need to heal a hurt.

That being said, some people in a moment are just not aware of how their behaviour affects others. Or some may feel elevated in their ego's state of self-importance or triumph if they've made a negative impact on someone else. While still others, if they do care about their negative impact, may be more invested in their ego's face-saving than stepping up to the plate and taking personal responsibility for their actions. In the end, how we demonstrate positive self-regard and attempt to respond to others without conscious injury is still our responsibility.

Forgiveness and acceptance can be practiced in a consistent way. I found that in order for me to maintain an open heart and peace of mind, I had to keep practicing forgiveness or giving up resentments *as soon as they arose*. A tall order at times, and I've had to keep working at it because I could feel that carrying resentment around was palpably disturbing for maintaining a calm mind.

Practicing forgiveness has helped me to change my perception and see that most people are doing the best they can, with whatever life has brought them, with whatever resources and ways of coping they have—or have not—learned. I cannot change what has happened, but I can change how I perceive the person, the situation and how I choose to manage my feelings.

Being Present

Being mindful and checking in to what I'm feeling in the moment, and what my needs are for good self-care, has helped keep me in the moment and has helped in reducing stress. Recognizing that the present holds the most potential for true power will decrease your anxiety. Re-focussing on the present becomes a habit with practice, and it works! Your inner quality of life will immediately improve with the present time focus.

Ego vs. Spirit

For years I have looked at how the ego plays itself out in my life. In any given moment, I'm either on a continuum with connection to my spirit in calmness and compassion, or I'm more responsive to my ego's issues related to the past or the future, with fear, anxiety or resentment.

We cannot feel love and fear at the same time. When we're fully involved in fear our egos cannot see or relate to the viewpoint of the higher spiritual self. The ego's demands for attention can become almost all consuming. It's insecure and always wants more answers in order to control outcomes. When we are connected to our spiritual nature we can perceive our ego's fears. At that point we can assuage its concerns with compassion and tenderness, simply by telling ourselves, "don't be concerned about it right now, we'll work it out."

The Mind/Body Connection

We are completely interconnected in mind, body and spirit, and our bodies transmit information to us every second.

Barbara Hoberman Levine (1991), in her book, *Your Body Hears Every Word You Say*, highlights the mind's impact on the body's functioning. She underscores the importance of understanding the body's response to the language we express about it on a daily basis.

When we speak in a way that tells our bodies we are lacking, unattractive or not valued, our bodies will hear us, just like any other person would hear us. It will be affected negatively or positively by our words and will respond in kind. We each strengthen our body's energy or we will weaken it.

Our bodies have their own consciousnesses and we are communicating with them constantly. When we realize this connection we can heighten our state of health and wellness.

Our bodies also give us messages in return regarding our own state of emotional and physical balance. Our minds can come up with dozens of interesting, fearful or misleading distractions for us at any given time, but it is our bodies that will always tell us the truth.

I noticed that whenever I was overly work-focussed and experiencing heightened stress, my response would tend to be to *work harder*. In those times, I perceptually became more tunnel-visioned and less open to my own spiritual guidance. I also manifested colds, flus and bouts of shingles. These events made me look at the entire mind/body connection more closely to see what I needed to change.

In considering my own involvement in a disease process, I did not see myself as a complete victim of an illness. Nor was it helpful for me to stand in judgment and blame myself for not doing enough of the "right" things to keep myself balanced and healed.

What I found helpful and effective was to get assistance to explore and learn what my body was trying to communicate to me with the illness symptoms. Whether we have knowledge of inheriting a predisposition to a particular disease or not, there are things that we can do to help ourselves in word, thought and deed to learn how to best manage any health issue. It has been helpful for me in learning and healing myself to appreciate what the traditional medical system has to offer as well as integration of other complementary therapies and spiritual healing methods. Addressing emotional and spiritual imbalances that can result in physical illness or disease requires mind, body, emotional and spiritual healing to fully address the illness. This holistic approach to treating illness leads to better preventative strategies and an improved quality of life.

On the whole, few people consciously wish to be ill. Illness does not immediately bring happiness or better quality of life. We can't always know each other's spiritual paths for learning and why things happen as they do. We are all unconscious of various aspects of ourselves. However, listening to our bodies and to our words and observing how our behaviours either create or assuage stress can help toward rebalancing ourselves and reducing the opportunity for disease.

In attending to our bodies' messages we can also learn about any connection to painful or traumatic past events, thereby providing another opportunity for clearing and healing.

<u>Journaling</u>

There are times in my life when I have communicated with my body through writing or journaling. I have simply asked why specific symptoms or illnesses were happening. As I allowed myself to be quiet and open, I would write down the information that would arise. I primarily found spiritual/emotional connections to my own past, to which my body was responding. My body was essentially telling me I was not treating myself well enough in aspects of my self-care, in that I was demanding too much from myself, thus creating even more stress. This imbalance was my own over response to a strong parental message about being responsible that was passed on to me in early childhood.

Any state of unbalance or disease gives us an opportunity to bring changes—changes that can be spiritually enriching and transformative in whatever the health outcome holds for us.

Let me tell you about my experience with Marlene. I met Marlene in Winnipeg while I worked at Evolve, a Domestic Violence Project, which helped abused women as well as men who abused their partners.

Marlene was a wonderful young woman with two small children. She had everything to live for and much to heal from. She had recently separated from her abusive male partner. Marlene explained she was a battered woman and a sexual abuse survivor, but she didn't want to participate in any group work. She wanted one-to-one counselling and wanted to talk and get her anger out.

Marlene also had breast cancer and it had metastasized to four of her ribs. Her throat was also being affected by the disease. Her prognosis was about two months left to live. Marlene refused radiation or chemotherapy. She was proud of her appearance and didn't want to lose it to the treatments. She was determined on this issue.

In the course of our discussion I asked Marlene about any spiritual beliefs that could help give her strength during this time. She said she didn't have any to speak of but was open to anything to lift her spirits.

I happened to have a couple of books on affirmations and creative visual work. Marlene bought her own copies of these books and proceeded to embrace their messages of the body, mind and spirit connection. She also used guided meditation tapes to communicate with her body and the disease. She wondered if she could heal herself.

On the third visit, Marlene asked if I would be an honorary pallbearer for her as she had few people that she felt she could ask. Obviously things didn't seem like they were going well for her, but she was still determined to carry on this path and embrace life to the fullest—going out to the best restaurants, doing everything that she was able to do and doing all the exercises she found in her books and meditations.

Marlene had to cancel her fourth visit with me due to her illness. She let me know she would get back. I did not hear from her for the next two months, save for a short voice message telling me she was still around.

Then Marlene called me. Her voice was distinctly different and she wanted to book another appointment. When she came in she had just been to her physician and she informed me she had gone into complete remission. I marvelled at her. She had gained weight and looked vibrant and healthy. I had not seen her look this well.

Marlene attributed her remission to the inner clearing she had done and all the affirmations and meditations she had committed to. She said she lived every day to the fullest. We had several more sessions and Marlene wanted to take a break and go forward on her own. She had done immense work, cleared a great deal and accepted her life's journey.

I ran into Marlene several times in the community before I relocated away. To my knowledge her life had gone forward in a positive way. She had met a loving man who was treating her and her children well.

Marlene's experience and outcome at the time I knew her is not everyone's outcome, but Marlene is a woman who affected my life with her courageous spirit. When I think of her she still reminds me about the power of steadfastly staying focussed in the moment and consistently affirming oneself with love and gratitude.

Masaru, a Japanese scientist, in his work, *The Hidden Messages in Water* (2001), suggests that words of love and gratitude have the power to create global change. What is so profound and simplistic in Masaru's work with water is his proof in showing us the impact of loving words on the molecules of water. Since our own bodies are composed primarily of water, it becomes a statement of immense importance to know we can significantly help ourselves and our bodies toward greater health, wellness and healing with words of encouragement, love and gratitude.

Treat your body as your very best friend and it surely will be.

Keeping a Positive Attitude

Positive energy attracts more of the same. Yet, how do we keep our positivity going when there is often so much negativity meted out to us? The media, with news about heart-breaking tragedies, lost lives, earth changes and the state of the world's economy, can relay the perception of a world on the brink of collapse. It can look dismal with messages relaying fear and scarcity.

In these moments I believe it is important to keep focussed on what we can first do individually that will contribute to positive regard and nourishment for ourselves. We give our best to others when we are first self-nourished. It's an excellent way to gently and powerfully combat the fear and negativity that we hear. Tuning out portions of the mass media's onslaught can be an initial step toward this end.

I think I've solved most of life's concerns sitting with my hairdresser, or sharing dinner with a dear friend. Some of the most positive people I know have dealt with incredibly painful, difficult life situations. They have survived and flourished in spite of what life has brought them because they resolved not to cave in to consistent pessimism, judgments and criticisms. Instead, they have continued to move themselves forward by focussing on what is positive and working well in their lives and what they are grateful for.

Positive energy can be built and reinforced over time. Small gestures matter. Anything you do, think or say that indicates goodwill toward yourself and nourishes you will immediately raise your self-esteem, increase your energy and carry you positively forward.

For example, I always feel immediately better and energized when I remember to just think well or compliment myself and others—when I eat or drink what I know is good for me, when I make efforts to get proper amounts of sleep and exercise, when I listen to good music and engage in positive conversations with others.

When you focus on what is positive, you will see that you can also positively magnetize situations you enter into with your very presence.

CHAPTER 6

TRANSFORMING TO WHOLENESS

I came here to spiritually evolve and to give service to humanity. The service I have given so far within the various roles as healer, Social Worker and teacher has been intertwined with my spiritual and personal growth. I will always want to be in the process of learning and growing no matter what role I am in.

The whole spectrum of experiences I grew up with has all been part of a grander design for me. Each experience, painful or joyful, became one I used to help me become self-reliant, more compassionate and more accepting. Even since my childhood, I wanted to be this kind of person because I have always believed in the strength and transformational power of Love. I wanted to be able to use my experiences to help people transition through difficult situations.

I'm someone who also relishes a good challenge and I took this life on with that attitude in most of the choices I made along the way.

Accepting Our Shadow Side

Accepting everything about myself has been revealing. I grew up well-trained as caretaker and rescuer. I had to therefore move myself away, step by step, to reverse parts of this conditioning. I had to consciously detach from others with acceptance and caring. I had to heal and re-balance myself; I had to learn how to give all the love and concern I'd willingly offered others right back to myself.

It's good to acknowledge our successes, our talents and our triumphs. It's also our choice to see our shadow side where our lack of self-love, fears and hurts can lie just beneath our awareness; or we can choose to not accept them. If we ignore this part of ourselves, though, I don't believe we can be as authentic in who we are and fully realize our true power—for human nature is one of duality.

Here is an ancient story, cryptically told with its dramatic emphasis regarding our duality:

In a Sumerian myth, Inanna and Ereshkigal were sisters. Inanna, the Queen of Heaven, left her place of the Holy Priestess of light and love, giving up all her power and worldly possessions. She travelled to the underworld to meet her sister, Ereshkigal, Queen and ruler of the Underworld.

In essence, Ereshkigal was the unconscious neglected side of Inanna; she was that part of Inanna that was unloving, unloved, abandoned, frightened, angry and lonely.

In order for Inanna to gain access to Ereshkigal, Inanna had to strip herself of everything she had ever known that could adorn and protect her, including her clothes. She had to come to her sister in naked humility.

This meeting did not fare well for Inanna. Ereshkigal in her jealously killed Inanna and hung her on a meat hook to die.

Over time, Ereshkigal came to mourn her sister and regretted that she willed her death. She realized that Inanna had been important to her. Ereshkigal missed Inanna's life presence and she fell into inconsolable grief.

Soon after, Inanna's grandfather, the God of Wisdom, was informed of Inanna's misfortune and sent two of his servants to the Underworld to speak with Ereshkigal. With compassion and empathy they approached Ereshkigal and asked her for what Ereshkigal really did not want to give away: her anger, despair and anguish, which she had projected onto her sister Inanna. They asked Ereshkigal for Inanna's body to return it to the upper world.

Ereshkigal finally consented to let go of part of her own unbearable pain and released Inanna. Inanna was eventually nourished back to life by the servants and rose to the upper world with the understanding that she could never forget her neglected, abandoned sister.

As Inanna carried the painful and frightening memories of her encounter with Ereshkigal to the upper world, her process of integration and transformation was realized. Inanna came to experience her true strength and power—the power that was born of pain and wisdom from descending and facing her sister, a part of her own self she had not recognized. (Sewell Ward, 2003)

Mirrors

We are given reflections of ourselves, through people and situations, to learn from. I can see that all through my life I have been placed in situations that directly mirrored back to me what I needed to learn or to heal from. Sometimes, I didn't like something in another person's personality because I didn't want to see that I had that very same trait within myself—a trait I had to accept.

In my professional capacities as a Social Worker I found myself in myriad positions where I was being continually confronted with my own history in working with abused and addicted people and those with mental health issues. These were all amazing and sometimes difficult opportunities for me to give service to others and to additionally heal myself.

Mirroring has also involved being able to appreciate my own strengths and gifts. Through the grace and teachings of others in my professional work and within my personal relationships, love, kindness, compassion, generosity and humour have all been reflected back to me.

Personal Responsibility

Being personally responsible to me means learning as much as I can about how I use my energy in the ways I communicate with people. I am always learning something new. Personal responsibility also means, to me, that I become aware of how I am contributing to the way my life is unfolding. Being personally responsibility for our lives means claiming our lives as we want them. It's still about how we are governing our energy in respecting ourselves, our resources, our homes, whom we choose to form close bonds with and how we nourish our minds, bodies and spirits.

Personal responsibility can involve leading by example. There tends to be a ripple effect on others in what we think, say and do. I heard good offerings years ago that essentially said that if you want to be recognized and appreciated, it's good to give that recognition and appreciation to yourself and to others. It will come back to you twofold. If you want to be strong and independent, decide to bring those qualities forward in yourself. Seek, read and practice the ways to enhance the strength that has already brought you this far. When you appreciate your own strength you will also see the strengths in others.

If you can, commit to increasing your practice in this area. When your mind is in gear in support of your feelings and wishes, you'll start creating the good habits that will reinforce your desired outcomes. If you need extra help, ask Spirit to head you in the right direction. Then if you wait a few minutes, you may feel a boost of energy to help carry you forward.

Intimate Relationships

Not everyone will choose to be in an intimate relationship and that is a viable choice. This choice has its own rewards. It has its challenges, too, in a world that emphasizes we are incomplete people if we are not coupled up. That view is false and spiritually undermining.

If we do choose to be in a personal relationship we can be confronted with some of our greatest hopes and fears. Intimate relationships always create opportunities for growth and healing. They can help us to evolve toward more compassion and unconditional love. They can also show us where we still need healing from past events or where our emotional growth has been restricted.

In relationships, when unhealed areas are exposed through our interactions, they can sometimes destabilize our relationships, particularly if we don't understand their source. For example, we all have a wonderful part of us, often referred to as our "inner child," that sparks fun, play and creativity in our relationships. For some though, if our inner child has been hurt in the past and if we have remained unhealed, this part of us can continue to interact with our partners from a wounded, sometimes destructive place that needs attention and healing.

Additionally, if we are still significantly unhealed from childhood wounds, we run the risk of choosing intimate partners who resemble those people that injured us. Often they've been our parents, siblings or any other key figure. Painful as it can be, this kind of involvement can provide an opportunity where we can choose to become more healed, stronger and decisive in closing the door that allows that kind of hurt back into our lives.

Fear of Love

People don't usually discuss "fear of love" as a general topic of conversation. We sometimes will refer to it as "fear of intimacy." Though we all seek love, many fear it to some extent, especially if there are still unhealed wounds or betrayals from family members or from intimate relationships.

Avoidance of love is also reflected in our English language, which tends to be quite violence oriented overall. We even choose terms like "non-violent" actions, rather than "loving or caring" actions.

The expression of love may not even be respected by some people as it can be seen as an attribute of weakness. It seems to me that deep down we know that love is a strong energy, an energy the world needs far more of.

In our personal relationships, if we do not yet appreciate that we are loving and loveable, we may not be as welcoming to love, comfort and caring when it is offered by another. It might feel too risky. For some people there might be a fear that they may have to live up to an expectation by another that they perceive is beyond themselves or deep down they may feel unworthy of love.

This fear of love may also be manifested in the need to control others and keep the caring they offer at a distance. There may be fear of letting one's guard down, becoming too vulnerable and perhaps becoming entrapped by another.

There may also be fear that certain personal "flaws" would be exposed and these perceived flaws would be found unacceptable by another. Many of these fears can become part of our own fearful projections or attributions and suppositions that can be made of others and that can result in shutting us down and keeping the love away we actually want.

In appreciating loving energy as it really is, it would tell us that it is not Love that has been injurious. It is the distortions, confusions and fears that have come through others' personalities and projections that have been wounding.

True loving spiritual energy is heart centred, and has strength. It has strength in the qualities of gentleness, truthfulness, acceptance, compassion, patience and endurance. It does not intend to injure or to control. It has the power to withstand the winds of change. This is the energy that is found in your own brave heart. When we are able to open our hearts to more gentleness, love and caring for ourselves, we gain in strength and openness to receive someone who embodies the caring qualities we deserve.

A healthy relationship is not with two "perfect" people; I don't know anyone like that, do you? When both people maintain their individual uniqueness, there can be growth in awareness regarding each partner's aspirations, needs and vulnerabilities. With continued respect for each other both people can create a stronger, more interdependent relationship of balance. Keeping open and keeping connected in mutual honesty invigorates growth and learning in our relationships.

A healthy relationship will still bring its share of challenges between two people. It can also offer freedom to be accepted just as you are.

There is a Rune called "Gebo" that stands for "Partnership, A Gift." It feels tender and freeing to me.

> *"I am your beloved,*
> *you are my true companion.*
> *We meet in the circle*
> *at the rainbow's centre,*
> *coming together*
> *in wholeness.*
> *That is the gift of freedom."*
> (Blum, 1989)

This freedom can come from choosing to see the love and goodness in yourself as well as in your partner. This recognition of your core essence, as being Love, can lead you to connect with the higher part of yourself—the higher part that knows the sacredness of life and sees Spirit in all that surrounds you. Strengthening this connection within yourself increases your connection to the Divine.

As we pay attention to the love that we are, we will see it grow stronger and become more a part of our intimate relationships. In this way you can also increase the strength and lovingness of your relationship.

A Higher Perspective

We are multi-dimensional beings with many aspects to ourselves. When we connect with the true spiritual essence of our Higher Self we are functioning at a higher vibration, a higher frequency. Our hearts become more open and we begin to see all situations from a greater place of acceptance and compassion. We are able to let go of our egos and our personality's issues and we can perceive the loving energy, Higher Power, the Buddha, the Christ or Allah within each person we meet. We can appreciate that every one of us wants to be loved, happy and respected regardless of our differences. From this higher perspective we can see our humanity's connectedness in that we are collectively part of a greater evolution of consciousness on this planet.

Perceiving life from this higher perspective involves our ability to maintain ourselves more in the present moment and allow others to be as they are. As we nourish ourselves toward a more loving, higher vibration, we will positively impact everyone around us. Their spirits will be uplifted. Moreover, our lives will flow more easily as our inner guidance, our intuition and other spiritual gifts will be increased and our creativity heightened. We'll have a clearer sense of our spiritual path.

As we all know, this is a time of tremendous conscious and systemic changes on our planet as our Earth spiritually and physically changes as well. Our Earth is also a conscious, spiritual energy form. We are interconnected and part of our Earth's transformation. This metamorphosis is also interwoven into our individual life paths. Some of us may have to relocate due to Earth's shifts and changes or we will have to move away from outdated institutions and systems that no longer work for us. It's important to keep listening to our guidance for direction in these changing times. By listening and following our inner spiritual voices, fears related to these dramatic changes can be diminished as different pathways are opened up for us.

I feel it is important to keep in connection with those you feel are your kindred spirits, those you most naturally resonate with. It's also important to know that your sense of community can be strengthened in each moment you give the gift of kindness and respect to another. Moving to resolve any outstanding differences or misunderstandings can also heighten your energy and help continue the healing for you and others.

Our time is short on this part of our journey together. Your power lies in your honesty.

I believe we are all here for a reason and we each have a special purpose and path. As you listen to your own spiritual guidance, you will come to discern your own spiritual voice of authority and you will be guided in a way that perfectly fits your circumstances.

As you keep opening to the strength and inner beauty of yourself you will see your own loving soul reflected back to you in nature, in events and in people who will come to support you on your life's journey. When you connect with the Divinity that surrounds you, the infinite intelligence of Spirit, you will see your deepest wishes come forward in the right time and in the right way.

Trust in your soul's wisdom and soon you will see yourself standing in your own light. For, truly, you are the Power, the Love and the Light; it has always been you.

EPILOGUE

LOVE IS BEING

This book was co-written with Spirit in a very short period of time. The information poured through me in a way that was as exhilarating as it was relentless. I felt that I almost had no choice but to just write; the feelings were so strong. I am grateful for the learning. I have transitioned through and resolved many things in life that it left room for me to clearly hear my soul's calling.

My connection with Spirit has been strengthened. I learned a long time ago in a spiritual group I attended that my spiritual expression in this lifetime was reflected in the phrase "Love is being." I've kept this phrase close in heart and mind because it meant I just needed to be myself, to just allow my own loving spirit to come through. The world at times does not make being our real selves easy, but it has been my spiritual challenge to allow this process to keep unfolding no matter what faced me. I have continued to grow in awareness of this heart-centred consciousness and it has brought me more peace and happiness.

My spiritual growth will always continue. More doors will open, more challenges will come and I will continue to want to give to others. It's been my lifelong passion to help myself and others appreciate how precious we are—no matter our status, capacity or role—and that we are, in heart and spirit, more powerful than we may know.

BIBLIOGRAPHY

Anderson, Susan. *The Journey From Abandonment to Healing*. Berkeley: Berkeley Publishing Group, 2000.

Beston, Henry. *The Outermost House: A Year of Life on the Great Beach of Cape Cod*. New York: Double Day and Company, 1928 (http://thinkexist.com/quotes/henry_beston)

Blum, Ralph. *The Book Of Rune Cards*. New York: St. Martin's Press, 1989; p. 129,175

Chopra, Deepack. *The Seven Spiritual Laws of Success. A Practical Guide to the Fulfillment of Your Dreams*. San Rafael, CA: Amber Allen Publishing and New World Library, 1994.

Deitz, Bob. *Life After Loss*. Tucson, Arizona: Fisher Books, 1988.

Dossey, M.D. Larry. *Recovering the Soul. A Scientific and Spritual Search*. New York: Bantam Book, 1989; p. 71.

Gawain, Shakti. *Creative Viuslization. Use the Power of Your Imagination to Create What You Want in Your Life*. Novato, CA: Nataraj Publishing, Div. of New World Library, 2002.

Graham, Helen. *Visualization. An Introductory Guide*. London, England: Judy Piatkus Publishing Ltd, 1996.

Hicks, Esther and Jerry. *Ask and It Is Given*. Carlsbad, CA; New York City; London, sydney,Johannesburg,Vacouver, Hong Kong, New Deli: Hay House, Inc., 2004.

Hoberman Levine, Barbara. *Your Body Believes Every Word You Say*. Santa Rosa, CA: Aslan Pulblishing, 1991.

Hopi Elder, unnamed. *A Hopi Elder Speaks*. Unknown. http://www.disclose.tv/forum/profound-prophecy-a-hopi-elder-speaks-t21132.html (accessed December 6th, 2010).

Miguel Ruiz, Don. *The Four Agreements*. San Raphael, California, Amber-Allen Publishing, 1997.

Niebuhr, Reinhold.1934, in "One Day At A Time In Al-Anon" Index. *Serenity Prayer*. New York: Al-Anon Family Group Headquarters, Inc, 1982.

Saint-Exupery, Antoine de (translation by Woods, Katherine, T.V.F.). *The Little Prince*. New York, USA: Reynal & Hitchcock, 1943; p. 70.

Seigel, Bernie, MD. *Love, The Healer, in Carlson, Richard, PhD and Shield, Benjamin. Ed. Healers on Healing.* Los Angeles: St. Martin's Press, NY, 1989.

Sewell Ward, Dan. *Library of Alexandria.* 2003. mhtml:// Interpretation of Inanna's Descent Myth (accessed January 09, 2011).

Silver Birch. *Teachings of Silver Birch (edited by A.W.Austen).* Oxshott, Surry. GB: Spiritual Truth Press, booksprint, 1938, 1998, 2008.

Wilde, Stuart. *Affirmations.* Taos, NM: White Dove International Inc., BookCrafters, USA, 1990.